AMAZING KYOTO

3.2million " 👍 Likes" from around the world

世界の320万人が " 👍 いいね！" した
「アメージング京都」

Discover Kyoto 編集部

はじめに

文化、伝統、芸術、1000年以上の歴史があふれる京都。京都に在住する外国人スタッフの「京都に伝わる美しい文化と芸術を世界中に広めたい」という想いから、2011年にFacebookのファンページ「Kyoto Fan」は生まれました。この4年間で、たったひとりだったスタッフが今では5人の外国人チームになりました。京都の美しい四季、歴史と物語を伝える寺社、日本人も知る人が少ない祭礼、京の美味。これらの写真、映像、情報を世界中の人々に向け、「Kyoto Fan」は発信しています。

毎週のように新しい発見があり、そのたびに私たちは京都の素晴らしさを感じています。ここでは一年365日、歴史と伝統にあふれるさまざまな行事があり、京都があらゆる顔を持っていることを知ることができます。世界中のファンが、この魅力に満ちた京都をシェアし、声を上げて喜んでくれていることは、私たちにとってもたいへん嬉しいことです。現在「Kyoto Fan」は、京都が大好きな320万人のファンとつながっています。こんなにも、ファンが増えていったことは、私たち自身も驚きを隠せません。「京都はアメージング！」、「京都に行くのが私の夢！」という温かい声を、アメリカ、オーストラリア、ベトナム…あらゆる国の数え切れないほどの方々からいただいています。

そして今年2015年、「今まで紹介してきた京都を一冊の本にまとめる」という、とても嬉しいオファーを小学館さんからいただきました。紙という、また違うメディアを通して、さらに多くの人に京都の魅力を伝えていけたらと思います。そして私たち「外国人チーム」の目から見た京都のひと味違う魅力を、日本人の読者の皆様に紹介するチャンスを与えてくださった寺社や取材先の方々にも心から感謝しています。

Discover Kyoto 編集部

最近は、取材先ともすっかり顔なじみになり、応援してくれる寺社も増えてきた。現在「Kyoto Fan」はFacebookのシティ部門で2位のパリ、3位のドバイを抜き、なんとファンの数が世界1位※。4年をかけて、思いがけないほど大きなファンページとなった。※Socialbakers調べ（Placeカテゴリ「City」でLike数世界1位／2015年8月現在）

They're becoming familiar faces around town, and the number of temples and shrines supporting them is increasing. The Facebook "Kyoto Fan" has surpassed #3, Dubai, and #2, Paris, to become the most popular "City" page on the site (according to Socialbakers, as of August, 2015). Over four years, the page has grown beyond expectation.

Prologue

Kyoto : the city with over a thousand years history as the center of culture, tradition, and arts in Japan. In 2011, Kyoto Fan was born in this city from the idea of a foreign employee in our company who desired to show Kyoto to the world. In four years time the Kyoto Fan team has grown from one to five international members. Using photography and videos, our mission is to share the beauty of Kyoto's four seasons, shrines and temples, festivals, and cuisine.

It's truly our pleasure to share this charming city with fans around the world, letting them experience the many sides to Kyoto in the form of its many historic events throughout the year. "Kyoto is so amazing!" "It's my dream to come to Kyoto!" People who live in other countries leave heartfelt comments that allow us to fully appreciate just how beloved Kyoto is. Even we have been surprised by the number of fans, with 3,200,000 people connected to Kyoto Fan from around the world!

In 2015, we were delighted when Shogakukan came to us with the offer to take what we had introduced online and turn it in to a book. We are incredibly grateful to have the opportunity to share information about Kyoto with even more people using this different form of media, as well as the chance to show Japanese readers just what it's like to see Kyoto through different eyes.

Discover Kyoto Team

取材ライターはニュージーランド出身のサラとアメリカ出身のエリザベス。フォトグラファーはベン、ビデオグラファーはディビッド。毎週2人1組で取材活動をしている。

The shooting team at work in Kyoto consists of writers Sara from New Zealand and Elizabeth from the United States, together with English photographer Ben and Australian videographer David.

今後は WEB サイト「Discover Kyoto」も発信予定。株式会社 俄の本社前で、マーケティング担当のティーラパットも交えて「Kyoto Fan」チームが勢揃い。

Their next project is the website, Discover Kyoto. Above is the team, including Thai marketing director Teerapat, in front of the Niwaka Corporation head office.

CONTENTS

[本書の使い方]
●マーク "いいね！" の数
Facebook「Kyoto Fan」ページ上で紹介した記事の中で5,000以上 "いいね！" がついた数字を載せています。コメントは、記事について世界中から寄せられたコメントの抜粋です。

●英文と日本文について
「Kyoto Fan」ページの記事は英文表記ですが、本書では英日併記しています。日本文は、日本人にあわせた内容に加筆、修正がされています。

●詳細データについて
掲載した日程、場所、出演者、料金、京の食の詳細は、2015年8月の時点での情報です。祭りやイベントの内容は毎年変わることがありますので、事前にチェックしてお出かけください。
食は季節や年ごとに内容や料金が変わりますのでご注意ください。
電話番号は日本からかけた場合の表記になっております。
海外からの場合は、＋81－市外局番（頭の0をはずす）－電話番号となります。

●インフォメーションについて
掲載しているHPのほとんどが、日本語のみの対応です。
英語対応をしている観光案内所や情報、Wi-Fi対応している場所の情報を巻末p193に紹介していますので、そちらをご覧ください。

[How to Use This Book]
● The Number of "Likes"
In this book, stories that garnered more than 5,000 "Likes" on Kyoto Fan's Facebook page have the number displayed. The comments on the stories are samples of those posted from all over the world.

● A Note on the English and Japanese Texts
Although Kyoto Fan's stories appear in English, in this book the stories appear in both Japanese and English. The Japanese versions have been edited and revised to make the content more suitable to a Japanese audience. Some romanization has been changed at the request of the rights holders.

● Regarding Listed Information
The data pertaining to the dates published, venues, speakers or performers, prices, and the details of menu items in Kyoto is current as of August, 2015. The particulars and contents of festivals and events are subject to change every year, so please be sure to confirm before you make any plans.

Please also be advised that the contents and prices of menu items are subject to change by the season or year.

The telephone numbers appear in a format for placing calls from within Japan. If calling from overseas, please use the following format: +81 - city code (exclude the starting 0) - phone number.

● Regarding English Support
Most of the websites appearing in this book offer only Japanese-language support. Please refer to page 193 at the end of the book for details on tourist information centers offering English-language support, other information in English, and places that offer Wi-Fi compatibility.

碑の穴をくぐったら、
願いごとを書いた
形代を貼り付ける!

世界の人が
最も"いいね!"した京都は!?

👍 64,844 いいね!
縁切り縁結び碑のある
安井金比羅宮!!

What aspect of Kyoto did the
people of the world "Like" the
most?
The Break Up/Make Up
Monument at Yasui
Konpira-gū!

祇園に安井金比羅宮という一風変わったご
利益のある神社があります。この神社は悪
い縁を断ち切ってくれることで知られてい
ます。神様の力により、人間関係や悪癖、病気、
悪い運気といったものを断ち切る願いが叶
うといわれています。境内にあるお札で覆
い尽くされた縁切り縁結び碑も有名です。
縁を切りたいものを書いた形代(かたしろ)
に覆われた白い佇まいは圧巻です。

At Yasui Konpira-gū, a shrine in the Gion
district that worships a god known for
his influence over the ties that bind,
there is a strange stone covered in
handwritten paper wishes. Take a bad
connection through the monument
with you and symbolically leave it
behind to come back through and free
yourself up to better things in life!

安井金比羅宮　住所→ p46
Yasui Konpira-gū　Address → pg.46

京の祭りには不思議な登場人物がいっぱい!!

Kyoto's festivals teem with mysterious characters!!

What is this?

一年中さまざまな祭りが行われている京都。そこでは歴史上の人物が登場したり、物語の中のキャラクターも描かれたりしています。華やかなコスチューム、独特の踊りなど見どころいっぱいです。

Held throughout the year, Kyoto's various festivals feature historical figures as well as recreations of imaginary creatures. There's so much to see, including their gorgeous costumes and unique dances.

迦陵頻伽
Karyōbinga

極楽浄土にすむ鳥。半身が鳥、半身が人間の姿。写真はいちひめ雅学会の演奏より(はねず踊りp104)。
Believed to live in paradise, Karyōbinga are depicted as half bird and half human (Hanezu Odori, pg.104)

空想上のキャラクター

Imaginary Characters

鬼 Oni

人々に厄や災難をもたらす鬼は敵役として登場(鬼踊りp82、やすらい祭p114)。
Oni play the villain, bringing about misfortune and calamities (Oni Odori, pg.82; Yasurai Matsuri, pg.114)

大蛇 Orochi

人々を苦しめる霊力のある大蛇(オロチ)(貴船祭p140)。
Orochi is a huge, evil snake with supernatural powers, stirring up trouble among people (Kifune Matsuri, pg.140)

白川女 Shirakawa-me
市中で花を頭にのせて売り歩いていた白川地方の女性（時代祭p34）。
The women from the Shirakawa region who walked around Kyoto city selling flowers held on their head (Jidai Matsuri, pg.34)

おひな様 Ohina-sama
ひな祭に登場する女びなで男びなと一対。十二単の姿の場合が多い（ひいな祭p94）。
The Empress who appears alongside the Emperor on Hina Matsuri, dressed in *jūnihitoe* (Hiina Matsuri, pg.94)

白拍子 Shirabyōshi
平安から鎌倉期にあった歌舞の一種、およびその舞女（はねず踊りp104）。
Poetic dancers from the Heian and Kamakura Period who performed in traditionally male clothing (Hanezu Odori, pg.104)

太夫 Tayū
江戸時代、美貌と教養を兼ね備えた最高位の遊女であったが、現在の太夫は島原太夫の文化を保存し継承する役割を果たす。写真は菊川太夫（義士会法要p62）。
The highest ranking courtesans of the Edo Period, endowed with both beauty and intellect (Gishi-e Hōyō, pg.62)

都を彩る
人物たち
The Colorful Characters of the Capital

童女 Warawa-me
幼い女の子。祭りの物語によく登場する（はねず踊りp104）。
Young girls who usually appear as court attendants (Hanezu Odori, pg.104)

侍 Samurai
戦国の武将も登場。写真手前は羽柴秀吉役（時代祭p34）。
Noble soldiers of the Sengoku Period. The man in the lead is the well-known Toyotomi Hideyoshi (Jidai Matsuri, pg.34)

鞍馬法師 Kurama-hōshi
鞍馬では武装した僧兵姿の法師が活躍した（竹伐り会式p152）。
The fierce warrior monks of Mt. Kurama (Takekiri-eshiki, pg.152)

山伏 Yamabushi
山野にすんで修行した僧。連絡手段に法螺貝を持っていたという（秋まつりp44）。
Yamabushi are Shugendō monks who train in the mountains and use conch shells to communicate with each other (Aki Matsuri, pg.44)

Some of the most iconic symbols of Kyoto are geisha, women who dedicate themselves to the preservation and performance of traditional arts and culture. Called *geiko* in Kyoto, these women live and work in five "flower districts" around the city, and girls who are studying their arts are known as *maiko*. Kofuku-san and Fukunae-san, two women working for the Shigemori Teahouse in Miyagawa-chō, kindly illustrate the differences between a *maiko* and *geiko*'s appearance.

MAIKO and GEIKO Differences

舞妓さんと

髪 Hair

舞妓さんは地毛で「割れしのぶ」の髪を結い、大きく派手なかんざしをつけます。
Maiko use their natural hair to form the *wareshinobu* style, and their *kanzashi* hair ornaments are large and colorful.

化粧 Make-up

「裾引き」の衣装を着るときは白塗りの化粧をします。眉と目は赤と黒の2色で化粧し、舞妓になった1年目は下唇だけに紅を入れます。
When in formal kimono, maiko paint their face white and use red and black to accent eyes and brows. A "small mouth" look is considered cute, so first year maiko paint only the bottom lip.

着物 Kimono

裾に綿をつめた「裾引き」と呼ばれる着物を着て、赤のちりめんに刺繍をした半襟をします。肩と袖には縫い上げがあり、これからまだ成長するという意味を持たせています。
Maiko wear embroidered collars that utilize the color red and special *hikizuri* kimono that were traditionally sewn to allow for growth spurts.

帯 Obi

舞妓さんは「だらり帯」と呼ばれる、後ろに長く垂れる特徴的な帯の締め方をしています。この締め方をするにはとても力が要るといいます。
Maiko have a very distinctive *obi* style called *darari obi*, which take a great deal of strength to tie.

おこぼ Okobo

5年寝かせた桐の木でつくります。高さは11〜12㎝で中には鈴が入っています。
Made of paulownia wood seasoned for five years, maiko wear 11-12 centimeters tall *okobo* that contain bells.

芸妓さん

どう違う？

京都の代表的なシンボルは芸者さんです。芸者とは伝統芸能と文化を継承し、演じることを職業とする女性のことです。京都では芸者は芸妓さんと呼ばれ、5か所ある「花街」で生活し、働いています。舞妓さんは修業中とされ、成長すると芸妓さんになります。写真の小ふくさんとふく苗さんは宮川町のお茶屋「しげ森」の芸妓さん（右ページ）と舞妓さん（左ページ）です。今回、おふたりに協力してもらい、芸妓と舞妓の違いを教えてもらいました。

髪 Hair

現代の芸妓さんはカツラをつけています。髪飾りはシンプル。
The more mature geiko use simpler hair accessories and typically use carefully styled wigs.

化粧 Make-up

「裾引き」の衣装を着るときは白塗りです。赤と黒の2色で眉と目と唇を描きます。
When in formal kimono, geiko may paint their face white and use red and black to accent eyes, brows, and a fuller lip.

着物 Kimono

舞妓さんから大人の芸妓さんになると「襟替え」をします。半襟の色が白になります。
When a maiko becomes an adult geiko, she undergoes the *erikae* and begins wearing a white collar.

履きもの Zori, Geta

芸妓さんの履きものは草履か下駄です。
Geiko footwear consists of low *zori* or *geta* sandals.

帯 Obi

芸妓さんの帯はお太鼓結びです。
Geiko tie their *obi* in the drum knot (*taiko musubi*) style.

Part 1

祭り、名所

Festivals, Famous Places

京都には 2000 以上もの寺社仏閣があります。

そして、そのひとつひとつが魅力的な歴史と行事を持っています。

京都で「何も行われていない」日なんてありません。

古い都でありながら、いつも新しいことが発見できるのです。

五穀豊穣や健康を願って行われる祭事は、世界中の人々の憧れの的。

街ごと伝統空間ともいえる京都で、日本文化の奥深さを感じてください。

Home to over two thousand shrines and temples, each with its own
fascinating history and yearly calendar of observances,
there isn't a day that goes by in Kyoto where there's nothing to see.
There's always something new to discover, even in the old capital.
The seasonal festivals, carried out in hopes of bringing about good
health and an abundant harvest of staple grains, are admired by
tourists from around the world. In Kyoto, where the town itself brims
with storied traditions of times past, penetrating insights into
Japanese culture await.

秋

Amazing
KYOTO

Autumn

京都の秋は、
真っ赤に色づいた紅葉の彩りと
夜のイルミネーションの光で
美しさに満ちています

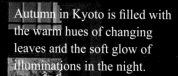

Autumn in Kyoto is filled with
the warm hues of changing
leaves and the soft glow of
illuminations in the night.

南禅寺塔頭・天授庵の夜の特別公開とライトアップ。白砂と苔の枯山水「方
丈東庭」のグラデーションが美しい紅葉の情景をつくりだします。
Tenju-an, a sub-temple of Nanzen-ji, hosts a special night opening
and illumination that showcases its gorgeous autumn scenery.

【南禅寺・天授庵】開催日程／11月15日〜11月末日
京都市左京区南禅寺福地町 86-8 ☎ 075-771-0744 17：30 〜 20：
45 料金／ 500 円 地下鉄東西線蹴上駅下車、徒歩7分。または
市バス南禅寺・永観堂道バス停下車、徒歩7分
【Nanzen-ji, Tenju-an】DATE：November 15 to November 30
86-8 Fukuchi-cho, Nanzenji, Sakyo-ku, Kyoto City 17：30 〜 20：45
Fee：500 yen http://nanzen.net

京都の秋は世界の人々を魅了するほどの美しさを誇ります。東山連峰に連なる古刹の庭は、秋の訪れとともに一層趣を増していきます。紅葉の景色にひんやりと冴えた空気、旬の食と相まって、古都の旅を思い出深いものにしてくれるでしょう。紅葉のベストシーズンは11月。歴史深い寺社や古い街並みを歩いて、自然の美しさをぜひ体感してください。とりわけ夜のライトアップで、色づいた紅葉が夜空に浮かぶ光景は幻想的。老若男女を問わず、多くの人々がこぞって訪れるのも納得です。紅葉の名所はたくさんありますが、特に永観堂、清水寺、南禅寺・天授庵のライトアップは圧巻です。

Kyoto is one of the best places in the world to experience a gorgeous autumn! Kyoto's beautiful temples, such as Nanzen-ji, Tōfuku-ji, and Kiyomizu-dera become even more amazing when the fall season arrives. The changing of the leaves, the brisk chill in the air, and delicious seasonal foods all combine to make a trip to the ancient capital an unforgettable event. Come to Kyoto to experience a journey filled with historic temples, stylish traditional streets, tasty treats, and breathtaking natural scenery. Conveniently accessible from both Tokyo and Osaka, the month of November is the best season of the year for viewing the vibrant red maple leaves in Kyoto.

p18／清水寺　p19 上／南禅寺・天授庵の庭　p19 下／永観堂
pg.18（top）：Kiyomizu-dera pg.19（bottom）：Eikan-dō pg.19（top）：
Tenju-an

【京都市内紅葉ライトアップ 開催日程】
ライトアップする寺院や開催日程は毎年変わるので、web をチェックしてお
出かけください。
問い合わせ／ http://kanko.city.kyoto.lg.jp/（京都観光 Navi）
【Kyoto Autumn Light-up Events】DATE
Light-up event dates vary by year. Check online to confirm.
http://kyoto.travel/en（Kyoto Official Travel Guide）
【清水寺】住所→ p26　【Kiyomizu-dera】Address → pg.26
【永観堂】開催日程／ 11 月初旬〜 11 月下旬（年によって異なる）
京都市左京区永観堂町 48　☎ 075-761-0007　17：30 〜 20：30 受
付終了、21：00 閉門
料金／ 600 円　地下鉄東西線蹴上駅下車、徒歩 15 分。または市バ
ス南禅寺・永観堂道下車、徒歩 3 分
【Eikan-dō】DATE：From early November to late November
（depending on the year）
48 Eikandō-chō, Sakyō-ku, Kyoto City 17：30 〜 20：30
Fee：600 yen　http://www.eikando.or.jp/

京都市内中心部から北西へ、車で30分ほどの距離ながら、市内とはまるで別世界のような雰囲気の高雄。高山寺、西明寺、神護寺といった美しい寺があり、紅葉のライトアップも行われます。

Located about 30 minutes away from the city center by car, the northwestern mountains of Kyoto can feel like a different world. Mt. Takao has beautiful autumn colors as well as three famous temples.

【高雄もみじライトアップ】開催日程／11月
年によって詳細が変わります。　JR嵯峨野線花園駅下車、
タクシーで約15分
JRバス～（約50分）～山城高雄・槇ノ尾・栂ノ尾
問い合わせ／☎ 075-871-1005（高雄保勝会）

【Takao Momiji Light-up Event】DATE：November
（Changes yearly）
☎ 075-871-1005（Association）
http://www.kyo-takao.com/light_up/

へ 舟遊び!

観月の夕べ 大覚寺
Kangetsu no Yūbe | Moon Viewing Party　　Daikaku-ji

大覚寺の大沢池は日本三大名月観賞地のひとつに
数えられ、素晴らしいお月見が楽しめる場所です。
Ōsawa Pond at the beautiful Daikaku-ji temple
is regarded as one of the three great moon-
viewing locations in Japan.

👍 29,641 いいね!

わぁ、美しい！ 日本に住んでいないのが
残念です。（カナダ）
Oh my gosh... That sounds SO
beautiful. Too bad I don't live in Japan.

The moon of the eighth lunar month is known in Japan for its particular beauty. In the Heian Period, moon viewing parties were a popular pursuit, with nobles throwing lavish banquets, leisurely sipping alcohol and composing poems together in competition on boats or moon viewing platforms. With over a thousand years of history, the moon viewing tradition still lives on in Kyoto.

Here you can enjoy a relaxed and cultural moon viewing at Daikaku-ji in Sagano. Participants may ride in ornately styled boats out on to the lake to enjoy the moon's reflection and the garden on the shore, as well as take part in a tea ceremony. Music is sometimes performed as well, and food stalls pop up near the pagoda. Once the sun has set and the moon has fully risen, Buddhist priests perform rites and offerings to the moon to pray for good harvests and happiness. This year there was a "concert" of sorts, with young monks singing the words of a classic sutra.

Held over several nights, those who wish to ride in the boats can buy tickets for 1,000 yen and choose between four time slots. Watching the full moon rise over the trees and cast its reflection on to the picturesque lake below is a beautiful sight to enjoy. Maybe you'll even be inspired enough to write a poem like the nobles of old?

八太陰月（西暦の9月）の満月は、特別に美しいことで知られています。平安時代（794年〜1185年）には、月見の会が盛んに行われていました。それは貴族の豪華な宴会で、美しい池で舟遊びに興じたり、月見のための特別な庭や月見台でゆったりと時間を過ごしたり…。そこで人々は酒を楽しみ、和歌を詠みました。現代のスタイルは少し変わりましたが、京の地には千年の歴史をもつ月見の文化がまだ残っています。

京都のさまざまな寺社では、この平安時代の月見会に似た十五夜の行事を楽しむことができます。なかでも嵐山の大覚寺で行われる「観月の夕べ」は有名です。大覚寺はもとは平安後期の上皇の宮殿でした。そしてその大覚寺よりも古いのが嵯峨天皇の時代につくられた大沢池です。参加者は舟に乗り、水面に映し出された月や池岸の庭、茶席などを楽しむこともできます。仏塔の近くには屋台も出ます。夕焼けを楽しみ、月が出たころ、僧侶は供物を捧げ、豊作と人々の幸せを祈願します。

この行事は、中秋の名月のころに3日間行われ、舟は17時から1時間ごとに数便出ます。当日でも乗船券を購入することができます。空にきらめく月と池に映し出される月は本当に美しいのひと言です。昔の貴族のように和歌をしたためてみるのも一興です。

【大覚寺】開催日程／中秋の名月のころ3日間
京都市右京区嵯峨大沢町　☎075-871-0071　15：00〜20：30（最終受付）
JR嵯峨嵐山駅下車、徒歩約17分。または嵐電嵐山駅下車、徒歩約23分
【Daikaku-ji】 DATE：3 days, during the harvest moon
Saga Ōsawa-chō, Ukyō-ku, Kyoto City　☎075-871-0071
http://www.daikakuji.or.jp　http://www.daikakuji.or.jp/english/ (English)

重陽の節句　上賀茂神社

Chōyō no Sekku | Chrysanthemum Festival　　Kamigamo Jinja

素晴らしい！ この文化は奥が
深くて、衣装も綺麗ですね！（チリ）
How wonderful! So full of
culture and beautiful costumes!

9月9日に菊酒を飲む儀式は、中国から伝わり
ました。十二単をまとった斎王代も陪覧します。
斎王代の従者「童女」（わらわめ）も辛抱強く
儀式を見守ります。
Drinking chrysanthemum sake was adopted
from a Chinese tradition of drinking
chrysanthemum wine on September 9th. The
woman dressed in the gorgeous layered kimono
is called the Saiō-dai.

Much as they do in the West, certain numbers hold significant meaning in Japanese culture. The number nine is considered to be an auspicious number by the Shinto religion, and based on that belief Kamigamo Jinja in northern Kyoto hosts the Chrysanthemum Festival (Chōyō no Sekku) on the ninth day of the ninth month, September 9th.

The Saiō-dai, a woman chosen to represent an imperial princess for the famous Aoi Matsuri festival, makes an appearance at the festival as part of her year-long appointment, accompanied by her young attendants and looking resplendent in classical multi-layered kimono. A rather interesting ritual takes place when priests from the shrine perform a prayer dance where they mimic crows, which are considered sacred at Kamigamo Jinja because of the legend of the three-legged *yatagarasu* who led the first Emperor. Those interested can also receive chrysanthemum *sake* from a shrine priestess. After the ceremonial portion finishes, local children compete in sumō wrestling matches called *karasu zumō*, or "crow sumō", which is a particularly popular event.

欧米で「7」が特別な数字であるように、日本にも特別な意味をもつ数字があります。たとえば神道では「9」がおめでたい数字とされています。上賀茂神社（京都にある世界遺産のひとつ）では、毎年9月9日に子孫繁栄と無病息災の願いが込められた「重陽の節句」が催されます。これは、9と9で二重におめでたいという意味が込められています。

世界遺産である上賀茂神社で、重陽の節句を見学する場合は、ぜひともカメラ持参で出かけてみてください。菊の花を浮かべた菊酒を飲んだり、ふたりの刀祢（とね）が烏（からす ＊上賀茂神社では神の使いとされています）を真似て飛び跳ねたり…と、興味深い儀式がたくさん行われています。菊酒を飲む儀式は中国の伝統が元になっていて、中国では9月9日に菊の花でつくったお酒を飲む習慣があったそうです。また神馬も一緒に飲みます（ただし、お水です…）。

また、有名な葵祭の主役である斎王代（さいおうだい）役の女性がまばゆいばかりの十二単姿で古式ゆかしく登場する様子も必見です。儀式のあとには「烏相撲」と呼ばれる子供たちの相撲の試合が行われ、境内はひときわ盛り上がります。

【上賀茂神社】開催日程／9月9日
京都市北区上賀茂本山339　☎075-781-0011　料金／無料　市バス・京都バス上賀茂下車すぐ
【Kamigamo Jinja】　DATE：September 9
339 Kamigamo Motoyama, Kita-ku, Kyoto City ☎075-781-0011
http://www.kamigamojinja.jp/event/sep.html
http://www.kamigamojinja.jp/english/index.html （English）

青龍会　清水寺
Seiryū-e | Dragon Parade　Kiyomizu-dera

👍 5,633 いいね！

僕は龍が大好きです！ 京都って
本当に素晴らしいところ！（アメリカ）
I love dragons,
Kyoto is an amazing place.

青龍は清水寺のある東山地区を守護しています。
青龍は東から来る災いから人々を守ります。龍
の動きに合わせて鳴らされる打楽器がにぎやか。
Seiryū is believed to protect the people from
misfortune coming from the east. The sound
of wooden clackers accompanied the dragon
as he flew through Kiyomizu-dera Temple.

Belief in the four divine god beasts of the cardinal directions is strong in Kyoto, and Seiryū the dragon is the guardian of the east. Considered a manifestation of the deity Kannon by Kiyomizu-dera, a famous temple located at the base of the eastern mountain range, Seiryū is celebrated in spring and autumn with the Seiryū-e Festival.

A relatively new festival by Kyoto standards, the Seiryū-e first began in 2000. The large dragon that appears in the parade, as well as the costumes involved, are all collaborations between famous costume designer Emi Wada and traditional Japanese artisans. Accompanied by the Four Heavenly Kings and other Buddhist divinities in Chinese-inspired attire, the dragon, covered in sutras and articulated scales, weaves and dances through the beautiful grounds of Kiyomizu-dera and into the surrounding neighborhoods, occasionally stopping to roar, pose, or peek into a shop. The temple is filled with the smell of burning incense, and the sound of traditional instruments being carried by the procession ring out over the assembled crowds. Watching the parade go by with the dragon seeming to glide through the air, it can feel as if the great blue dragon has come down from the mountains to survey his domain.

龍というと少し怖いイメージがありますが、風水では守護神とされています。「青龍」と呼ばれる巨大な龍は、京都を守護する四神のうちのひとつです。東の方角を守るこの龍に敬意を表して、清水寺では「青龍会」という祭事が、3月と9月の春と秋にそれぞれ2日間、また4月に行われています。ここでは、龍は観音（慈悲の神）の化身であると信じられています。

2000年に始まったこの祭りは、京都では比較的新しい行事です。青龍をはじめ、人々の幸せを祈る夜叉神、青龍を守護する四天王など、さまざまなキャラクターが華やかに登場します。行列に登場する巨大な龍と神の使者・眷属（けんぞく）の装束はすべて世界的デザイナーであるワダエミさんと、伝統工芸作家のコラボレーションから生まれました。

古い時代の中国の戦士と巫女から着想を得たという装束に身を包んだ男女が、経文が書かれた鱗に覆われた龍を担いで、清水寺から門前町を練り歩きます。寺の境内はお香の香りで満ち、眷属たちが見物客に向かって打ち鳴らす伝統楽器の音が響きわたります。まるで天空から舞い降りてきたかのような龍の行列を見ていると、青龍もこのような祭事が行われることを喜んでいるかもしれないと思えてきます。

【清水寺】開催日程／毎年5日間　3月14日、15日、4月3日、9月14日、15日
京都市東山区清水1丁目294　☎ 075-551-1234
14：00 ～　市バス五条坂下車、徒歩10分
【Kiyomizu-dera】DATE：5 days every year, March 14, 15, April 3, September 14, 15
1-294 Kiyomizu, Higashiyama-ku, Kyoto City　☎ 075-551-1234　14:00
http://www.monzenkai.com/seiryue.html
http://monzenkai.guide-book.jp （English）

鞍馬の火祭 由岐神社
Kurama no Hi Matsuri | Fire Festival　　　Yuki Jinja

大人用の松明は 80kg以上あり、男たちが苦労して担ぎ上げる様子から、どれほど重いかが窺えます。
The large pine torches carried by adults weigh more than 80 kilograms. You can really see how heavy they are if you watch how much effort the men have to put in to lift them.

素敵な思い出が蘇りました！京都が恋しいです！私の夢の町です！（イスラエル）
Thank you for bringing up a beautiful memory - I miss Kyoto - the city of my dream!

The Kurama Fire Festival is one of the most famous fire-based festivals in Kyoto and also considered one of its most eccentric. Based on the journey of the god Yuki Daimyōjin to Yuki Shrine on the slopes of Mount Kurama in 940 after a series of disasters in the capital, the main draw of this festival is the procession through the village of Kurama of local men bearing huge flaming torches.

When the sun sets, watch fires are lit in front of homes and torches are readied, with the large *taimatsu* carried by adult men weighing up to 80 kg! The torch bearers gather at the steps leading up to the Sanmon Gate, and when the festival reaches its peak more than a hundred are assembled. Once the sacred rope is cut, select men make their way up the mountain to retrieve two portable shrines, which are then paraded around the village with the bearers showing their strength along the way. The local men wear traditional garb that includes warrior's sandals, a loincloth, a skirt made of braided rope, an armguard made from colorful patterned fabric, and a padded cloth slung over one shoulder to lay the torch on. Lasting until midnight in the still warm October weather, the Kurama Fire Festival is a remnant of a different time where it's easy to lose yourself in the fervor of the night.

有名な「鞍馬の火祭」は、毎年10月22日に京都北麓にある由岐神社で行われます。そのスケールの大きさや賑わいなどについて、ある程度は心構えはしていたとしても、きっと想像以上に驚いてしまうでしょう。早めに鞍馬に着こうと、早い時間帯の電車に乗っても、すでに同じような計画の観光客でいっぱいのはずです。多くの外国人観光客の姿も見られます。クラシックな外観の叡山電鉄の車窓の景色を眺めながら、満員電車に揺られるうちに、祭りの興奮が高まっていきます。

午後6時、家々の前に篝火が灯されます。ひと晩中続く行列では、老若男女関係なく全員が装束を着て松明（たいまつ）と神輿を担ぎます。燃え盛る松明を持った村人が声を合わせて、「サイレイ、サイリョウ（祭礼や、祭良）」と声明（しょうみょう）を唱え、山上の由岐神社の神輿を担いで、夜の集落を練り歩きます。村の人は年齢に関わらず参加し、地域社会が一体となって祭りを盛り上げます。大人用の松明は重さ80kg以上もあり、屈強な男性たちも持ち上げるだけで大変そうです。

鞍馬の火祭は、平安時代に朱雀天皇（すざくてんのう）によって、鞍馬山の由岐神社に神を勧請（かんじょう ＊お迎えする意）した際の行列を再現したといわれています。一気に赤く燃え上がる多くの松明には感動すら覚えます。村人の声と炎の熱気に包まれた10月の夜は、忘れられない思い出になるでしょう。

【由岐神社】開催日程／10月22日
京都市左京区鞍馬本町1073
料金／無料　叡山電鉄鞍馬駅下車、徒歩10分
【Yuki Jinja】DATE：October 22
1073 Kurama-honmachi, Sakyō-ku, Kyoto City　Fee：Free
http://www.yukijinja.jp

義経祭 鞍馬寺

Yoshitsune-sai | Martial Arts Festival　　Kurama-dera

祭りの間、幼少期の義経の人形が本殿に置かれ、
天狗の絵が描かれた木板も見受けられます。日本
舞踊や合気道などが奉納されます。
A statue portraying the young Yoshitsune at the
age when he lived at Kurama-dera is enshrined
in the main hall during the festival.

 11,044 いいね！

義経様は僕のヒーローです。（イギリス）
Yoshitsune sama is a personal
hero of mine.

Minamoto Yoshitsune is well known in Japanese history as a heroic warrior. Around 1159 the young Yoshitsune was sent by the Taira clan to Kurama Temple, where it was deemed he would pose no threat after his father's assassination. Instead, he trained, some say with a mountain *tengu*, and came back to take his vengeance on the Taira. However, he was eventually embroiled in a power struggle with his brother and betrayed. His legend lives on, though, and Kurama-dera holds the Yoshitsune Festival in September to honor him.

Within the main hall a special portrait of Yoshitsune was on display for the memorial service as incense and sutra chanting filled the air. Because it was where he spent time honing his martial prowess, the main public event of the festival is a martial arts demonstration of *aikidō* performed on the main temple steps. Offered up to the deities of the temple, there is usually a dance dedicated to his memory featuring music and the *tengu* with which he purportedly honed his skills.

For those interested in history or martial pursuits, take this opportunity to enjoy a journey up to Kurama Temple and observe a quiet festival where you won't feel crowded out. Try to imagine how Yoshitsune's childhood might have been at this scenic Buddhist sanctuary!

日本の歴史上で、「源義経」の名はよく知られています。義経は1159年に生まれ、父・義朝が暗殺されたあと、敵側の平氏によって、幼少期に鞍馬寺へ預けられました。そこで義経は修行し（天狗から武芸を学んだという伝説もある）、兄の頼朝、家来の弁慶と共に平氏を滅ぼし復讐を果たしました。しかしその後、頼朝との政権争いに巻き込まれてしまいます。藤原氏に寝返られ、義経は家族を殺され、自刃し果てました。彼の伝説や武勇伝は今でも語り継がれ、幼少期を過ごした鞍馬寺では9月に義経祭が行われます。

義経祭の日は、源義経と彼の思い人で人気の白拍子（しらびょうし）であった静御前の法要が行われます。本殿の中にはお香の香りが漂い、経を読む声は重く響き渡ります。特別に展示された絵には、いまもなお語り継がれる伝説の義経が生き生きと描かれ、絵の義経は、まるで参拝者を見つめているかのようです。義経が鞍馬寺で武術を練習していたことにちなみ、本殿の階段では合気道の奉納も行われます。よく天狗と太鼓の舞が奉納されますが、取材した年には、日本舞踊と琴の演奏が行われました。

静かで神聖な雰囲気をもつ鞍馬寺。いつ訪れても自然に囲まれた鞍馬寺からの風景はとても美しいので、ここで育った義経の幼いころに思いを馳せながら、訪ねてみてはいかがでしょうか。

【鞍馬寺】開催日程／9月15日
京都市左京区鞍馬本町 1074　☎ 075-741-2003
11:00 ～　料金／300円　叡山電鉄鞍馬駅下車、徒歩 30 分
【Kurama-dera】 DATE：September 15
1074 Kurama-honmachi, Sakyō-ku, Kyoto City
☎ 075-741-2003　11:00　Fee：300yen

上京薪能　白峯神宮
Kamigyō Takigi Nō | Firelight Theater　　Shiramine Jingū

白峯神宮での能はさまざまな人々の舞台が
見られるとてもよい機会です。
The *nō* performance at Shiramine Shrine
is a good opportunity to see the masters
and apprentices at work.

素敵!（沖縄）Gorgeous!

The oldest form of Japanese theater still performed, *nō* (or noh) is a complex art that utilizes masks, costumes, a small orchestra, chanting, fans, and gestures to tell a story. The themes in *nō* are often supernatural, dealing with deities, demons, warriors trapped in hell, and the ghosts of women tormented by love. Developed in the 14th century, this slow and graceful stage art is most commonly identified by its haunting wooden masks. Several schools maintain the ancient traditions, and *nō* is often performed as an offering to the gods during religious ceremonies and events.

In late September, Shiramine Jingū, a small shrine in Kyoto's Kamigyō Ward, is host to the annual Kamigyō Takigi Nō performance. Takigi Nō, or "Firelight Nō", is performed throughout an evening on a lit open-air stage. At this performance, various *nō* schools, a *kyōgen* troupe, *hōbu* dancers, *koto* players, and other musicians all gather to entertain the audience. Beginning from 4pm and lasting several hours with an intermission in between, the Kamigyō Takigi Nō serves as a great chance to experience a variety of traditional Japanese performing arts of all levels of mastery. If you have a chance, visit Shiramine Shrine and enjoy the supernatural allure of *nō* by night.

現代に残る最も古い伝統芸能のひとつである「能」は、14世紀室町期に始まりました。面、装束、扇を用いた型、囃子、謡…などさまざまなものを構成して舞い語られますが、最も特徴的なのは「能面」でしょう。能のテーマには、神、亡霊、修羅に落ちた武士、愛に生きる女性が登場します。現在では、観世流をはじめとする流派や一家が能の伝統を受け継いでいます。芸能として舞台で演じられていますが、儀式や祭りの奉納として演じられることもよくあります。

白峯神宮では、「上京薪能」（かみぎょうたきぎのう）が行われます。薪能は、夜、ライトアップされたなかで行われる屋外の舞台のことを指します。上京薪能では能だけでなく、狂言、日舞、琴の演奏など、いくつかの伝統芸能が披露される貴重な機会です。薪に点火され、白峯神宮の神職が儀式を行ったあと、いくつかの流派が舞台に登場します。取材した年は、「京鹿子娘道成寺」、続いて琴の演奏、大蔵流狂言の茂山家の「鬼瓦」、夜の最後に「猩々乱（しょうじょうみだれ）」が演じられました。

ちなみに白峯神宮には、崇徳（すとく）天皇、淳仁（じゅんにん）天皇が祀られています。また境内には、平安時代のスポーツである蹴鞠（けまり）の守護神・精大明神が祀られています。そのためスポーツの神社として知られ、多くの有名なサッカー選手が参拝し、蹴鞠も奉納行事として行われます。

【白峯神宮】開催日程／9月下旬
京都市上京区飛鳥井町 261　夕方〜　薪能／有料　市バス堀川今出川下車すぐ
問い合わせ／上京区役所地域力推進室 ☎ 075-441-5040
【Shiramine Jingū】DATE：Late September
261 Asukai-chō, Kamigyō-ku, Kyoto City　From the evening
Event Fee：Applies ☎ 075-441-5040 （Kamigyō City Hall）
http://www.kyoto-kankou.or.jp/event/

時代祭
京都御所〜平安神宮
Jidai Matsuri | Festival of the Ages
Kyoto Gosyo ~ Heian Jingū

Japanese Beauty !

時代祭では、平安時代の姫君をはじめ、
歴史を彩ったさまざまな美しい女性に
扮した人たちが登場します。写真は、
旅装束姿の平安貴族の女性。
Beauties from the various periods of
Japanese history, such as this
traveling Heian Period noblewoman,
assemble for the Jidai Matsuri.

行列が始まる前に京都御所で儀式
が行われ、時代衣装をまとった
2000人以上が参列します。
Before the procession begins, a
ritual is dedicated in front of the
old Imperial Palace. This year
around 2,000 people participated
in the procession!

 8,287 いいね!

写真がすごすぎる！ 興奮する！ 人の笑顔、表情、行列の
光景も圧巻！ 素晴らしい！
The pictures are mind blowing!! You've managed
to capture some brilliant smiles and expressions
and people and perspectives! Great job!!

Considered to be one of the top three festivals in all of Kyoto, Heian Shrine's Jidai Matsuri (Festival of the Ages) is held on October 22nd each year. Heian Shrine was built in 1895 to commemorate the 1,100th anniversary of the founding of Kyoto as the capital of Japan, while the Festival of the Ages was started as a celebration of Kyoto's history and to honor two emperors connected with unifying the country.

The festival is composed of a two kilometer, five hour long procession of volunteers dressed in historical garb representing Japanese history from the Meiji Era all the way back to the Enryaku Era in the 780's. Painstakingly recreated and researched, even making and dyeing the fabric using techniques from a thousand years ago, the procession is akin to watching a living history museum march by. Not only do famous lords and princesses make appearances, but warriors, priests, politicians, merchants, and commoners are all represented, giving a very comprehensive look into the appearance of Japan past.

The parade begins at 12 pm and makes its way from the old Imperial Palace to the site of the Heian Shrine. Paid seating is available at three different locations along the route, and information is available in pamphlets so that you know just who is passing by!

京都三大祭のひとつ、平安神宮の「時代祭」は毎年、10月22日12時から行われます。東京遷都で天皇、皇家、政府が東京に遷られたあと、残された京都の人々は京都を復興するため、1895年、平安遷都1100年を記念として、当時の大内裏の一部を復元しました。これが平安神宮です。時代祭は、京都の歴史を振り返り、祭神である桓武天皇と孝明天皇をお祝いするために生まれた祭りです。

時代祭は2kmの道のりを約5時間かけて、さまざまな時代装束（780年ころの延暦年間から明治時代）に身を包んだ人々が練り歩き、歴史を再現する祭りです。参加者たちは、まるで博物館から抜け出してきたようです。歴史上の人物やお姫様だけではなく、武士、神職、政治家、町衆なども登場し、その時代衣装から日本のこれまでの装束や着こなしなどがわかります。しかし、なんといっても歴史上の有名な人物たちを見られるのが魅力的です。落ち延び姿の常盤御前（ときわごぜん ＊義経の母）、女武芸者の巴御前（ともえごぜん）、歌舞伎をつくった出雲の阿国（いずものおくに）、悲劇の姫君・和宮（かずのみや）、桓武天皇、織田信長の列には羽柴秀吉（のちの豊臣秀吉）、維新勤皇隊など顔ぶれ豊か。

行列は12時にスタートし、京都御所から平安神宮まで進みます。ゆっくり座って見学したい人は有料の観覧席（御所、御池通り、平安神宮の3か所）もあります。

【時代祭】開催日程／10月22日
京都御所／京都市上京区京都御苑 3、平安神宮／京都市左京区岡崎西天王町
☎ 075-761-0221 (平安神宮)
【Festival of the Ages】DATE：October 22
Kyoto Gosyo：3 Kyoto Gyoen, Kamigyō-ku, Kyoto City
Heian Jingū：Okazaki Nishitennō, Sakyō-Ku, Kyoto City ☎ 075-761-0221 (Heian Jingū)
http://www.kyokanko.or.jp/jidai/

笠懸神事 　上賀茂神社
Kasagake Shinji | Horseback Archery Ritual 　Kamigamo Jinja

神事としての馬上の弓術の始まりは、欽明
（きんめい）天皇のころ。笠懸神事は2005
年に復活。競技は南北に立つ2名が扇子を
上げて確認し合いながら進められます。
The use of mounted archery as a ritual can
be traced all the way back to the reign of
Emperor Kinmei. After an 800 year hiatus,
this Kasagake Ritual was revived starting
from 2005.

奇跡的にこのすごいイベントを見ることができました。
ハラハラしました！
I was privileged to see this wonderful
championship of skill, it was breathtaking.

038

Performed at Kamigamo Shrine in October, Kasagake Archery is one of the three original styles of archery performed for the entertainment of the deities in Japan. The nature of the shooting at this event harkens back to the practice drills performed by archers in the days of Japan's Warring States Period, recreated as part of a religious offering.

This ritual is performed by the Takeda-ryū school of mounted archery. As opposed to the more common *yabusame*, where the archers shoot at one fixed target, the archers at this event take aim at five targets (three at shoulder height and two closer to the ground), to simulate more realistic military maneuvers on the battlefield. Hits are announced after each run, and riders with the highest score advance to the second round, where the targets shrink in size. Watching the riders race down the trail while drawing back their arrows before letting them fly was exhilarating, especially when they found their mark!

Held at Kamigamo Shrine on the third Sunday in October, this event begins at 12:30 pm, with the archery portion taking place from 1:00 pm. As commentary is provided in English, it is easy for tourists to understand the events. Take a look for yourself and marvel at the beauty of the horses and riders at the Kasagake Shinji!

10月に上賀茂神社で行われる「笠懸神事」は、奉納行事として行われる弓術のひとつで、歴史はとても古く800年前にさかのぼります。興味深いこの神事は、弓術を受け継ぐ武田流により行われます。武田流の宗家は50代目で、その歴史は清和天皇の息子、貞純親王（873〜916）までさかのぼります。

この弓術は、昔の武士の練習の形と似ています。ひとつの的を狙い射る流鏑馬（やぶさめ）とは違い、笠懸神事は肩の高さでふたつ、低い位置で3つ、全部で5つの的を射るという戦場に近い状況の中で競技が行われます。騎手は赤い顔の鬼神のついた烏帽子（えぼし）を被り、射るときに使う5つの矢を持っています。初戦から勝ち上がった騎手と馬は、2回戦ではさらに小さな的を狙い、勝者を決めます。この小さな的は丸い陶器で紙吹雪が入っており、紙吹雪が落ちないと当たったとは認められません。駆ける馬、馬に乗りながら弓を引く騎手、そしてとりわけ放たれた弓が的に的中する瞬間は迫力ものです。

笠懸神事の歴史や実況は英語でも説明されます。上賀茂神社で、笠懸神事の騎手と美しい馬をぜひご覧ください。

【上賀茂神社】開催日程／10月第3日曜日
京都市北区上賀茂本山339 ☎ 075-781-0011 料金／無料
市バス・京都バス上賀茂前下車すぐ
【Kamigamo Jinja】 DATE：3rd Sunday of October
339 Kamigamo Motoyama, Kita-ku, Kyoto City ☎ 075-781-0011
http://www.kamigamojinja.jp/topics/2014/2014_kasakake.html
http://www.kamigamojinja.jp/english/index.html （English）

ずいき祭（瑞饋祭）　北野天満宮
Zuiki Matsuri │ Harvest Festival　Kitano Tenman-gū

900年半ばごろに始まったという祭り。少女たち
は八乙女舞を奉納します。大人と子供が一緒に踊
り、祭りに参加する光景に心が和みます。
The festival is believed to have started in the
mid 900's. Young girls performed a traditional
offering called the Yaotome Dance.

綺麗なところ！ 綺麗な人たち！（イギリス）
Beautiful place. Beautiful people xx

The five day Zuiki Matsuri is said to have a thousand year history, tracing all the way back to the mid-900s, inspired by a procession linked to the Kitano Tenman-gū deity and to expressing gratitude for bountiful harvests. The procession departs from the shrine on the first day, carrying with it several *omikoshi*. After making its neighborhood rounds, the parade arrives at a temporary shrine where rituals are conducted, including the Yaotome Dance performed by young girls. After a three day period, the portable shrines are all carried back to Kitano Tenman-gū in a parade with ox-drawn carts, with the ceremonies concluding the next day with a final dance offering.

The most eye-catching aspect of this festival, however, is the *omikoshi* decorated with vegetables and dried foods. Starting with a wood base, taro stems (*zuiki*) are used for the roof, and dried greens, marigolds, tofu skin, and wheat bran serve to cover the rest of the surface. On each side, art panels are constructed depicting legendary scenes or creatures using vegetables and rice, and strings of colorful dried scarlet eggplant, citrus, and peppers hang as decorations off each corner. With that kind of portable shrine, it's easy to see how this event is one of the most iconic autumn festivals in Kyoto.

芸妓、獅子舞、稚児(ちご ＊寺で働く小姓)、平安時代の宮廷装束、野菜の神輿などなど。これら色とりどりのキャラクターに共通することは、すべて「ずいき祭」に登場するということです。いったいだれが1000年も前にこんなことを思いついたのでしょう？

ずいき祭は10月1日から5日までの5日間、北野天満宮で行われる秋の収穫祭で、収穫した米の籾殻、野菜、果物などを奉納し、神に感謝を捧げる祭りです。祭りの初日、天神様ののられた御鳳輦(ごほうれん)が北野天満宮の御旅所(おたびしょ ＊祭事中の神の仮安置所)に運ばれ、3日後に元の神社に戻されます。そして、この御鳳輦の往復に、にぎやかな行列が従います。

最も目を引くのはやはり野菜と乾物でできた神輿です。屋根はずいき(里芋の茎)で葺かれ、それ以外の部分も、干し菜、マリーゴールドといった花々、湯葉、麦の穂などで覆われています。側面には、物語の場面や神話に登場する生き物が野菜で表現されており、四隅には紫色の干しなすび、柑橘類、唐辛子などがカラフルに飾られています。ずいき祭が京都を代表する秋祭りのひとつに数えられるのも、この御鳳輦を見ればよくわかります。10月1日、御鳳輦が御旅所に到着した際に行われる儀式を着御祭、10月4日の行列は還幸祭といい、行列は北野天満宮周辺の住宅地にも練り歩きます。

【北野天満宮】開催日程／10月1日〜5日
京都市上京区馬喰町　☎ 075-461-0005　市バス北野天満宮下車すぐ
【Kitano Tenman-gū】DATE：October 1 to 5
Bakuro-chō, Kamigyō-ku, Kyoto City　☎ 075-461-0005
http://kitanotenmangu.or.jp/

亥子祭 護王神社

Inoko-sai | Young Boar Festival　　Go'ō Jinja

かわいいね！
（オーストラリア）
Kawaii neee！

女性たちは、まるで平安時代
を舞台にした映画の登場人
物のようでした。
The ladies look like they
are straight out of a Heian
Period movie.

The Inoko-sai (Young Boar Festival) held each year at Go'ō Shrine is a sacred ritual started by the emperor during the Heian Period. Traditionally, it was held on the first day of the boar in the tenth month of the lunar calendar, a day when it was said that by eating mochi you could ward off all manner of sickness and misfortune. This special treat is called *inoko mochi*, or "young boar mochi", which also has implications for propagating a large family. Specially made with flour containing seven different ingredients (soy beans, azuki beans, black-eyed peas, sesame, chestnut, persimmon, and rice sugar), the *mochi* is shaped around red bean paste and formed in to the shape of a boar.

Reenacting the ritual once held in the Heian court, several women dressed as *nyōbō*, high ranking court women, carry the tools to make *mochi* to a room in the shrine where the chief priest awaits. Dressed as a Heian Period emperor, the chief priest pounds the rice cakes into *mochi*. After the *mochi* has been prepared, the group receives lanterns and proceeds with a crowd behind them to the nearby Imperial Palace, where they offer up their prayers. For those interested in trying *inoko mochi* themselves, it is sold at Go'ō Shrine during this festival!

「亥子祭（いのこさい）」は平安時代に宮廷が取り入れた年中行事で、毎年11月1日に護王神社で行われます。これは陰暦10月の初亥にあたり、この日に餅を食べるとあらゆる病気や災いから身を守ることができると信じられています。この餅は「亥子餅」と呼ばれていますが、これには多産のイノシシのイメージから子孫繁栄の意味が込められています。米粉に7種類の粉（大豆、小豆、ササゲ、胡麻、栗、柿、糖）を加えてつくった亥子餅は、中に餡を入れてイノシシの形に整えられています。

儀式は平安朝の宮廷行事を再現したものです。まず宮廷の高級女官である女房に扮した女性たちが拝殿に餅つきの道具を運びこみ、平安朝の帝に扮した宮司が餅をつきます。それから一同は提灯をさげ、行列をなして神社からほど近い京都御所へ移動し、そこで祝詞（のりと）を捧げるのです。どの女房たちも優雅で美しく、雅な印象です。

この日に食べると、翌年は病気をしないという亥子餅。亥子餅は祭りの期間中、護王神社で販売しています。

【護王神社】開催日程／11月1日
京都市上京区桜鶴円町385（烏丸通下長者町下ル）
☎ 075-441-5458
【Go'ō Jinja】 DATE：November 1
385 Ōkakuen-chō, Kamigyo-ku, Kyoto City
http://www.gooujinja.or.jp/

秋まつり 狸谷山不動院

Aki Matsuri | Fall Festival　　Tanukidanisan Fudō-in

Traditionally, the changing of the seasons is celebrated with rituals that usually focus on praying to cleanse oneself of past wrongs and for blessings in the future. In this vein, Tanukidanisan Fudō-in Temple celebrates its Fall Festival in early November. The Aki Matsuri involves visitors writing their wishes on wooden tablets, and monks, who practice a form of mountain asceticism called *shugendō*, throwing those wooden tablets into a sacred bonfire. With the sound of Buddhist sutras in the air, the wishes of the participants are blessed as they are engulfed in the fire.

新しい季節を迎えることは、神道でも仏教でも、どちらにとっても重要なテーマです。11月3日、狸谷山不動院を訪ねてみましょう。自然に囲まれた境内は幻想的な空気に包まれ、参道のいたる所に狸の置物が並んでいます。狸谷山不動院の「秋まつり」で行われるのは、氏子や一般の参拝者が願いごとを書いた護摩木（ごまぎ）を、修験道（しゅげんどう）と呼ばれる山岳信仰の修法を修めた僧が火に投げ込んで焚き上げる儀式です。独特の節まわしで経を唱えながら、炎に飲み込まれる護摩木のひとつひとつに祈りを捧げます。この日は、先着1000名の参拝者に力団子が振る舞われます。その名の通り、新しい秋を迎えるにあたり、力と強さを与えてくれるものです。

【狸谷山不動院】開催日程／11月3日
京都市左京区一乗寺松原町6
☎ 075-722-0025　市バス一乗寺下り松町下車、徒歩15分
【Tanukidanisan Fudō-in】DATE：November 3
6 Ichijōji Matsubara-chō, Sakyō-ku, Kyoto City　☎ 075-722-0025
http://www.tanukidani.com/

梵燈のあかりに親しむ会 　東林院

Bontō no Akari | Illumination　　Tōrin-in

Usually off-limits to walk-ins, the private Myōshin-ji sub-temple Tōrin-in opens its gates to the general public for the Bontō no Akari. The Bontō no Akari is a candlelight festival that involves 400 candles, lanterns, and other lights set up around the temple garden, illuminating it as night falls. These lights make the whole temple seem to glow and creates a magical atmosphere for visitors to walk around and enjoy. Compared to other more bustling festivals, the Bontō no Akari is a simple affair that allows one to appreciate the beauty of nature, silence, and flickering light.

妙心寺の塔頭（たっちゅう）寺院のひとつ、東林院はふだんは非公開の寺ですが、毎年10月半ばに開催の「梵燈のあかりに親しむ会」の会期中は一般拝観できます。

400本のろうそく、灯籠、その他の照明が夜の境内をロマンティックに照らすライトアップイベントです。地面に並べられたろうそくの様子を見ていると、「月は天下の秋を知る」という一節が心に浮かんできます。ろうそくのほのかな灯りは、シンプルながらも、自然の美しさや静けさを感じさせてくれます。枯山水の庭を眺めながら、抹茶と和菓子をいただくこともできます。有名な 「沙羅双樹の庭」 を見るのもお忘れなく！

【東林院】開催日程／10月第2金曜日から10日間
京都市右京区花園妙心寺町 59
☎ 075-463-1334　市バス妙心寺前下車、徒歩 6 分
【Tōrin-in】 DATE：10 days from the 2nd Friday in October
59 Myōshinji-chō, Hanazono, Ukyō-ku, Kyoto City　☎ 075-463-1334
https://kanko.city.kyoto.lg.jp/

櫛まつり 安井金比羅宮

Kushi Matsuri | Comb Festival　　Yasui Konpira-gū

各時代の髪型と時代衣装を着た40人ほどの女性が行列に参加。和装姿がとてもエレガント。「黒髪」という舞踊が奉納として踊られます。
Over forty women participate in the parade of hairstyles, each also wearing clothing appropriate for the period she represents. The women are pictures of elegance.

👍 7,281 いいね!

皆すごーく綺麗です！
私も自分の着物が欲しい！（ハンガリー）
They are all soooo very beautiful!
I wish I had some kimono of my own.

A small shrine in the Gion area most famous for its powers over the ties that bind, Yasui Konpira Shrine traces its history back to the late 600's and enshrines a famous warrior, an emperor, and the serpentine water god Ōmononushi no Kami.

There is a legend that features Ōmononushi hiding within a woman's comb case, and due to this association a burial mound for combs was erected on the shrine precincts. Called the "*kushizuka*", this mound was created in order to honor combs and hair ornaments once they were no longer needed, rather than discard them like trash. As a "thank you" to these items and supported by a beautician's association, Yasui Konpira Shrine hosts its annual Kushi Matsuri, or Comb Festival, every September.

After an explanation and the addition of new combs to the grave, the festival kicks off with the classic dance "Black Hair". Once the ceremonies are completed, a parade of women representing hairstyles and ornamentation from the 6th century all the way to the present makes its way around the area in a walking timeline. Members of the Kyoto Beauty Culture Club toil to painstakingly recreate the hairstyles as faithfully as possible using the women's natural hair— which is quite a feat, considering how elaborate the styles of the past could be!

縁結びと縁切りで有名な神社、安井金比羅宮は7世紀、藤原家の寺として創建されました。時が経つにつれて寺社の目的が変わり、忘れられていた時期もありましたが、1695年に現在の姿となりました。境内には、武将で歌人の源頼政、島流しになった崇徳天皇、蛇神であり水神の大物主大神（オオモノヌシノカミ）が祀られています。

大物主大神は蛇の姿で女性の櫛箱に隠れたという伝説があり、その繋がりで1961年に神社内で櫛用の土饅頭「櫛塚」がつくられました。櫛塚は使用しなくなった櫛を敬うための場所です。その櫛への感謝の気持ちと美容師の活躍を祈り、安井金比羅宮では毎年9月に「櫛まつり」を行います。

祭りの午後、櫛塚の前で儀式が始まります。神主は儀式を説明し、櫛を櫛塚に入れます。本殿の前で舞妓による「黒髪」の舞踊が奉納されます。儀式と奉納が終わると、和装姿の女性たちが集まり、伝統的な結び髪を披露しながら、祇園界隈を巡ります。古墳時代から現在まで、それぞれの時代ごとの結び髪を再現しているので目を凝らして見てください。蔓を頭に巻いた縄文時代、中国の影響を受けた奈良時代の古い髪型から、宮女官見習いの髪型、室町時代の庶民の髪型、遊女のヘアスタイルまで、興味深い髪型ばかりです。

参加した女性たちは、京都美容文化クラブのメンバーです。昔の髪型は複雑ですが、本当に美しいことがわかるでしょう。

【安井金比羅宮】開催日程／9月第4月曜日
京都市東山区下弁天町70　☎ 075-561-5127
13:00〜　京阪祇園四条駅下車、徒歩約10分。
市バス東山安井下車、徒歩約3分
【Yasui Konpira-gū】DATE：4th Monday of September
70 Shimobenten-chō, Higashiyama-ku, Kyoto City　☎ 075-561-5127　13:00
http://www.yasui-konpiragu.or.jp/　http://www.yasui-koupiragu.or.jp/en/（English）

人形供養　宝鏡寺

Ningyō Kuyō │ Doll Memorial Service　　Hōkyō-ji

京都の人形の職人と店主は、この儀式に参加し、供養を終えるまで人形を見守ります。取材した年は、島原太夫の文化を継承する女性のひとり、菊川太夫も登場しました。
Doll craftsmen and shop owners from all over Kyoto volunteer at this event, seeing their creations through to the end.

👍 9,722 いいね!

この大事な思いがこもった文化を教えてくれてありがとう。（アメリカ）
Thank you for sharing this caring & sensitive custom with us.

The "Doll Temple" Hōkyō-ji, a nunnery usually open only twice a year for doll exhibitions, also holds a special Doll Memorial Service in mid-October.

In Japan there is a belief in a kind of spirit called "*tsukumogami*". These creatures are believed to be created when an item reaches one hundred years of age, and items made in the shape of a person are believed to be particularly capable of gaining a "soul". On that basis, and with support from the Kyoto Doll Commerce & Industry Cooperative, Hōkyō-ji holds its Ningyō Kuyō to soothe the spirits of dolls that are no longer needed or that have become weathered and worn.

For the ceremony, the nuns of the temple assemble before the Doll Burial Mound, and a *tayū* from Shimabara makes a rare appearance to preside over the ritual, along with women dressed as imperial princesses. The women present prayers, incense, and flowers in front of the burial mound before the nuns begin the Buddhist service. Finishing with a dance and song performance by the *tayū*, everyone is left feeling that the dolls will be respectfully seen to. If you have a doll that has served you well in the past and you think it would be a shame just to throw it away, look into a memorial service send-off in Kyoto!

「人形寺」と呼ばれている宝鏡寺は尼門跡寺院で、昔は代々、皇女が住持として勤めました。御所からきた皇女は、父君である天皇から季節の変わり目や祝いごとがあるたびに人形が贈られていたことから、現在もここには当時の姫君たちの人形が多数所蔵しています。1年に2回、春と秋に開催される人形展では、それらの人形が一般公開され、「人形供養」が行われています。

昔の日本では「付喪神（つくもがみ）」の存在が信じられていました。人々が使う物は100年経つと妖怪である「付喪神」になってしまうと信じられていたのです。とりわけ人形は「付喪神」になりやすいといわれ、魂が宿ると考えた人もいました。そのような考えから、京人形商工協同組合が中心となって、必要とされなくなった人形の「魂」を弔うため、ここ宝鏡寺で供養を行うようになりました。儀式を通して持ち主は感謝の意を込めて人形の魂を送ることができます。

尼僧たちは人形塚の前に集まります。現在では珍しい島原の太夫も奉納を行うため登場し、皇女役の女性ふたりも装束を着て参加します。太夫と女性たちは祈り、花と香を供えて、尼僧が供養を始めます。供養が終わると、太夫が舞いを奉納します。

ちなみに、人形塚には武者小路実篤が詠んだ歌碑が寄せられています。その碑には「人形よ　誰がつくりしか　誰に愛されしか　知らねども　愛された事実こそ　汝が成仏の誠なれ」と書かれています。

- -
【宝鏡寺】開催日程／10月14日
京都市上京区百々町547（寺之内通堀川東入ル）
☎ 075-451-1550　10:30〜1時間　市バス堀川寺之内下車、徒歩約1分
【Hōkyō-ji】DATE：October 14
547 Dodo-chō, Kamigyō-ku, Kyoto City　☎ 075-451-1550　10:30
http://www.hokyoji.net/

火焚祭 伏見稲荷大社

Hitaki-sai | Fire Festival　　Fushimi Inari Taisha

 6,440 いいね!

来年の夏、京都を訪れるときに
伏見稲荷大社に行くのが楽しみです。
（アメリカ）
I will be visiting Kyoto next
summer and cannot wait to
see the Inari Shrine.

熱い炎に向かって火焚串の束を投げ込みます。
収穫のため里に降りていた穀霊神（こくれいし
ん）を冬の間に山にお送りする意味が込められ
ています。
It's said that this ritual and the fires call Inari
to come back to the mountain to rest for the
winter after it's hard work in the rice fields
during the harvest.

The head shrine for the 30,000-plus Inari Shrines around the country, Fushimi Inari attracts a great number of visitors from around Japan, with many coming to Kyoto to participate in the Hitaki Fire Festival.

The first part of the ritual begins in the shrine's main hall with offerings of food, drink and prayers while priestesses perform a sacred *kagura* dance for the gods. From there, everyone moves to a clearing where three bonfires are waiting to be simultaneously lit. When the smoke clears, priests begin throwing bundles of prayer sticks into the fires in large, dramatic tosses, scattering the wishes of Inari shrine visitors in the flames. A copy of the purification prayer is passed out in the crowd, so any attendee can join in wishing for everyone's good health and fortune, as well as the country's prosperity.

The heat and flames provide a dramatic backdrop as priests undertake cleansing rituals in front of each fire, using water, salt, and *sakaki* leaves, and sacred *kagura* dances are performed intermittently by priestesses carrying golden bells until the last prayer stick is tossed in to the fire. Held in autumn, it's said this ritual fire calls Inari back to the mountain from the fields to rest after harvest— and it certainly called to us as well!

京都のみならず、世界で最も有名な神社のひとつである伏見稲荷大社では、11月の初旬、秋の収穫が終了したころ、いよいよ「火焚祭」の時期がやってきます。

伏見稲荷大社は国内に3万もある稲荷神社の総本宮として、日本全国はもちろん、海外からも多くの参拝者がこの行事に参加するために訪れます。火焚祭は本殿の祭りから始まります。そこで神主が食物をお供えします。宮司が祝詞を読み、神楽たちが雅楽の調べにのせて神楽を舞ったあと、神主が本殿内に集まった参拝者を稲荷神のもとへと導きます。

午後から神主と参拝者は、3つの火床（ひどこ）が準備された神苑斎場に行きます。神主は火床の前に水、榊（さかき）、塩を置いて祓いをし、金色の鈴を持つ神楽たちが神楽を奉納します。皆が集まったら火床が燃やされ、神主は全国の参拝者が奉納した十数万本の火焚串の束を投げ込み、伏見稲荷大社の参拝者の祈りを込めて燃やします。大祓詞（おおはらえのことば ＊唱えれば唱えるほど功徳が増す）の最後の言葉で行事が終わります。

大祓詞が書かれた紙は、皆に配られますので、神主だけではなく参加者も一緒に罪障消滅（ざいしょうしょうめつ ＊己の罪を治癒させること）、万福招来を祈りましょう。

【伏見稲荷大社】開催日程／11月8日
京都市伏見区深草藪之内町68
☎075-641-7331　13:00 〜　料金／無料　JR稲荷駅下車すぐ
【Fushimi Inari Taisha】DATE：November 8
68 Fukakusa Yabunouchi-chō, Fushimi-ku, Kyoto City　13:00　Fee：Free
http://inari.jp

鎧着初式　上賀茂神社
Yoroikizomeshiki | Armor Procession　Kamigamo Jinja

> すごく綺麗でカラフルな
> 衣装ですね。（日本）
> Very pretty and
> colorful costumes.

行列は境内を歩き、一の鳥居をく
ぐって本殿へと向かいます。子ども
からお年寄り、幅広い年齢の人々が
参加しています。
The participants parade out of the
shrine grounds and then in through
the main gate. From the young to
the old, you can see different
generations participating in this
event.

The Yoroikizomeshiki ritual held at Kamigamo Shrine may not have a thousand years of history, but this festival, begun in 2008, has become popular as an occasion where families dress in samurai armor together in order to pray for the good health and growth of their children. Sponsored by Usagi Juku, an armor manufacturer, the Yoroikizomeshiki is based on a time-honored tradition of becoming a man in a ritual where boys would don their first pair of armor- though these days, both boys and girls participate.

Using lacquer paper connected with cords, participants carefully create the detailed armor and helmets they and their children or grandchildren will wear and then join in a procession at Kamigamo Shrine in late November, where prayers are conducted to wish for the health, growth, and good fortune of the young. With their colorful armor set against brilliant autumn foliage, the festival members both young and old are transformed into splendid samurai, who can be seen making their way through Kamigamo Shrine's grounds to a purification in front of the main hall before heading inside for further blessings. If you have the time, you might want to try a hand at making a set of armor yourself or simply enjoy watching the procession pass on by.

両親に手伝ってもらい凛々しい鎧装束に身を包んだ子どもたち。颯爽とした姿も美しい女性たち。これは、鎧製作工房の鎧廼舎うさぎ塾が主催して執り行われている上賀茂神社の「鎧着初式」の光景です。2008年に始まった新しい行事ですが、鎧甲の武者姿のパレードは男女問わず大人から子どもまで参加できる大人気のイベントです。2015年10月には、21年に1回の上賀茂神社の式年遷宮に合わせて大鎧だけの特別な儀式も行われます。

この儀式は、その昔、若者が初めて鎧を着る日を祝う元服が元になっていますが、現在は年齢に関係なく参加できます。参加者は紐のついた漆紙を使って鎧をつくり、自分や子ども、孫に着せて、上賀茂神社での行列に加わります。また神社では子どもたちの成長、健康、幸福を祈願する祝詞が捧げられます。カラフルな甲冑が鮮やかな秋の紅葉に映え、老いも若きも、みな侍気分を味わえます。

主催のうさぎ塾では手づくり甲冑教室も開いていますので、興味のある方はぜひサイトをのぞいてみてください。

【上賀茂神社】開催日程／11月23日
京都市北区上賀茂本山339　☎075-781-0011　市バス・京都バス上賀茂前下車すぐ
【Kamigamo Jinja】DATE：November 23
339 Kamigamo Motoyawa, Kita-ku, Kyoto City　☎075-781-0011
http://www.usagijuku.com/（うさぎ塾）

Make a Wish!

京都で願いごとを叶えましょう！

地主神社（じしゅじんじゃ）は、清水寺の境内の中にあるひっそりとした神社です。しかし、その歴史は古く、創建年代は「神代（かみよ）」（日本の建国以前）とされ、現在の社殿は1633年徳川家光公により再建されたものです。京都の長い歴史を見守り続けてきた地主神社ですが、ここが多くの人で賑わうもうひとつの理由があります。それは、この神社が良縁の神様・大国主命（オオクニヌシノミコト）を主祀神とする"恋愛の神社"として名高いからです。ここには、恋の願いが叶うと伝わる「願掛けの石」がふたつあり、片方の石からもう一方の石へ、目を閉じながら歩き、辿りつけると恋が叶うといわれています。

Jishu Jinja, nestled inside Kiyomizu-dera grounds, is a shrine rich with history. The shrine is famous for match-making and couples. There are many ways you can make wishes to strengthen your love fortune. You can write wishes on tablets, or even try walking between two love rocks.

"Love!" 恋愛の神様
地主神社

有名な「恋占いの石」。写真はもみじ祭のときのもの。人を象った紙に息を吹きかけ、身代わりとして水に流し、悪運、悪縁など災難除けの「人形祓い」も有名です。
The famous love rocks. The Momiji Matsuri at Jishu Jinja. Write your love wish... Then set it free in the water.

【地主神社】
京都市東山区清水 1 丁目 317 ☎075-541-2097
「五条坂」「清水道」各バス停で下車、徒歩 10 分
【Jishu Jinja】
1-317 Kiyomizu, Higashiyama-ku, Kyoto City ☎075-541-2097
http://www.jishujinja.or.jp/

Good Luck Charm!

お守りに注目！

1. For Headache

頭痛封じ　三十三間堂

Zutsū Fūji
Sanjūsangen-dō

柳は昔から頭痛を防ぐ漢方薬として有名です。三十三間堂の重要な行事である楊枝のお加持では、聖樹とされる「楊枝・やなぎ」て、観音様に祈願した法水を参拝者に注いで、諸病を除くという儀式が行われます。この行事にちなみ、境内の柳の木と秘呪「消伏毒害陀羅尼」を収めた「頭痛封じ」という名前のお守りがあります。

This charm filled with a piece of willow and a sutra is said to aid in preventing and curing headaches. Willow has been used in folk medicine to soothe headaches for centuries.

2. For Scholastic Success

学業成就　黄檗山萬福寺

Gakugyō Jōju Omamori
Manpuku-ji

宇治市の黄檗山（おうばくさん）萬福寺には、鉛筆の形の学業成就のお守りがあります。五角（合格）鉛筆の五色セット。五教科「数学、理科、社会、国語、英語」の向上を願うお守りです。ここでは変わったお守りがあるだけではなく、坐禅、写経、普茶（ふちゃ）料理なども体験できます。

This charm is geared towards helping you in your studies. The five pencils represent the five main subjects in school— Math, Science, Social Studies, Japanese, and English.

3. For Break Up/Make Up

縁切り＆縁結び　安井金比羅宮

Enkiri/Enmusubi Omamori
Yasui Konpira-gū

祇園の安井金比羅宮は、主祭神の崇徳天皇（すとくてんのう）が讃岐の金刀比羅宮で一切の欲を断ち切ってこもったことから、古来、断ち物の祈願所として、人々が悲しい境遇にあわぬよう悪縁を断ち切る神社です。ネガティブな関係から縁を切る「縁切り」と、良縁と良い生き方を応援する「縁結び」のお守りがあります。

The first charm, "*enkiri*" ("bond severing"), serves to let you break free from negative relationships. The second, "*enmusubi*" ("bond securing"), allows you to make good ones.

【三十三間堂】
京都市東山区三十三間堂廻町 657
☎075-561-0467　京都七条駅下車、徒歩7分
【Sanjūsangen-dō】
657 Sanjūsangen-dō Mawari-chō,
Higashiyama-ku, Kyoto City　☎075-561-0467
http://www.sanjusangendo.jp

【黄檗山萬福寺】
京都府宇治市五ケ庄三番割34
☎0774-32-3900　JR奈良線黄檗駅、京阪宇治線
黄檗駅下車、徒歩5分
【Manpuku-ji】
34 Sanbanwari, Gokashō, Uji City, Kyoto
☎0774-32-3900
http://www.obakusan.or.jp/
http://zen.rinnou.net/head_
temples/02manpuku.html（English）

【安井金比羅宮】
京都市東山区下弁天町 70
☎075-561-5127　京阪祇園四条駅下車、徒歩10分
【Yasui Konpira-gū】
70 Shimobenten-chō, Higashiyama-ku,
Kyoto City　☎075-561-5127
http://www.yasui-konpiragu.or.jp/
http://www.yasui-koupiragu.or.jp/en/（English）

冬

Amazing
KYOTO
Winter

冷たい風と、時おり舞い降りてくる雪が
都の風情と相まって、
美しく静かな冬の表情をつくり出します

Crisp winter winds and the
occasional snowfall turn
the old capital in to a serene
winter landscape.

霧に包まれた嵐山。うっすら雪の積もる冬のある日、一艘の
舟が保津川を渡ります。冬の幻想的なシーンも感動的です。
Arashiyama's mountains and the Hozugawa River are
wreathed in mist and a fine layer of snow as a boat
makes its way across the water.

嵐山花灯路 嵯峨・嵐山周辺
Arashiyama Hanatouro | Illumination   Saga, Arashiyama Area

ライトアップされた嵐山はとてもロマンティックで、その美しさは言葉で言い表せないほど。渡月橋も感動するほど美しく見えます。
An illuminated Arashiyama creates a romantic and somber atmosphere. The Togetsukyō bridge looks absolutely amazing.

花灯路を見に行ったことがあります。雪も降っていました。素晴らしかったです。（オーストラリア）
I have seen the Hanatouro Festival, once in the snow, and it's very special.

For ten days in December, the mountainside area of Arashiyama in western Kyoto is brilliantly illuminated with lanterns and lights that arc through trees and bamboo to make an amazing nighttime sight: the Arashiyama Hanatouro Festival.

Starting at 5pm, the lights turn on and the early winter evening is brightened until 8:30pm with several temples and shrines along the light-up route holding special night openings for tourists. The most popular public areas, such as the Togetsukyō Bridge and Bamboo Forest, are lined with lights and more artistic works of arranged lighting and painted lanterns. You can even find large works of *ikebana* flower arrangements placed here and there along the way.

Around 5 kilometers of pathways are wired up for the "Light and Blossoms Pathway". From the Hankyu Arashiyama Station you can head to Hōrin-ji and see kaleidoscopic projections on the temple or head over to the riverside park with art displays and pale orange lights shining on the famous Togetsukyō. Over the river you can continue on to the awe inspiring bamboo forest, where you can visit Nonomiya Shrine or Ōkōchi Sansō Villa. Moving deeper into the Saga area leads to the temples Jōjakkō-ji and Nisōn-in, as well as the poet's hut Rakushisha, all of which are illuminated and awaiting your visit!

12月中旬の10日間、「嵐山花灯路」が開催されます。散策路に沿って置かれた露地行灯が、山の木々や竹林を照らし、素晴らしい夜を演出してくれます。冷たい冬の空気と相まってため息が出るほど美しい光景を見ることができます。初冬の夕暮れを照らす点灯は、17時から20時30分まで。期間中は沿道の寺院や神社のいくつかでは、夜間特別拝観が行われています（一部、昼の拝観終了後、再度開門の場合も）。昼間の嵯峨・嵐山の素晴らしさは言うまでもありませんが、夜もまた違った味わいがあります。渡月橋（とげつきょう）や竹林などがスポットライトでライトアップされ、さらに「京都いけばな協会」による大きないけばな作品も展示されています。

全長約5kmの「灯りと花の路」は、阪急嵐山駅から出発します。十三まいりで有名な法輪寺では、建物の壁に万華鏡のように映し出された光のアートが施されます。また河川敷には、学生によるアート作品も飾られています。オレンジの灯りに照らし出された渡月橋を眺めながら、いよいよ竹林の小径へ。温かな自然光や白色などに照らされてまっすぐ伸びた竹林の小径を歩いて行くと、野宮神社や大河内山荘庭園にたどり着きます。この大河内山荘庭園あたりで引き返す人も多いのですが、さらに嵯峨野の奥に足を延ばすと、常寂光寺や長神の杜（ちょうじんのもり）のほか、松尾芭蕉ゆかりの落柿舎（らくししゃ）など風情のある名所旧跡でもライトアップがされていますので、ぜひ訪れてみてください。

【嵯峨・嵐山】開催日程／12月中旬〜10日間（年によって異なる）
京都市右京区嵯峨中ノ島町付近　17:00〜20:30（2015年）
料金／散策無料（拝観料等別途必要）　JR嵯峨野線・嵯峨嵐山駅、阪急嵐山駅下車
問い合わせ☎075-212-8173（京都・花灯路推進協議会事務局）
【Saga, Arashiyama】DATE：10 days from mid-December（Changes yearly）
Near Saga-Nakanoshima-chō, Ukyō-ku, Kyoto City　17:00〜20:30（2015）
Entrance Fee:Varies by Temple　☎ 075-212-8173（Comittee）
http://www.hanatouro.jp/arashiyama/　http://www.hanatouro.jp/e/arashiyama/index.html（English）

山科義士まつり 山科一帯
Yamashina Gishi Matsuri | 47 Rōnin Festival　Yamashina Area

赤穂浪士が勢ぞろい

行列は山科の毘沙門堂から出発し、終点の大石神社まで約4時間かけて練り歩きます。四十七士には山科区民が扮しています。
The procession departs from Bishamon-dō on the north side of Yamashina Ward.

ぼくは真剣道を学んでいるので、この記事に興味を持ちました！ありがとう。（アメリカ）
Because I do Shinkendo,
I was very interested in this. Thank you.

Celebrating the history of the 47 Rōnin, a tale said to embody the samurai code of honor, the Gishi Matsuri is held on December 14th each year in Yamashina, starting from the Bishamon-dō temple. According to the story, the *rōnin* were left masterless when their lord was forced to commit suicide as punishment for an indiscretion against an official. The samurai could not allow the stain to remain on their dead lord's reputation, so after laying low and planning for years, the warriors infiltrated the official's estate and succeeded in killing him. After taking his head to their lord's grave, the warriors turned themselves in. Because they had acted to restore their lord's honor, they were allowed to commit suicide rather than be executed, solidifying their role in Japanese legend.

The main event of the Gishi Matsuri is a parade that involves participants dressed in traditional clothing and armor walking through the neighborhood, re-enacting the day the *rōnin* set out for Tokyo to get revenge. Partway through their journey the group stops at a stage where there are performances by a *taiko* group, as well as reenactments of famous scenes from the 47 Rōnin story, skillfully done by TOEI actors, before the group prays at Ōishi Shrine for the repose of the honorable departed.

12月14日、山科一帯では、山科区民が手づくりで行う「山科義士まつり」が行われます。「忠臣蔵」で有名な四十七士は、山科と縁が深く、大石内蔵助（おおいしくらのすけ）が隠棲した岩屋寺に近い大石神社では内蔵助をお祀りしています。また毘沙門堂は当時の門跡公辨法親王（こうべんほっしんのう）が、四十七士の処分について、将軍綱吉に意見を求められ、武士としての切腹を注進、これにより綱吉は切腹を命じたと言われています。

忠臣蔵とは、武士道精神を体現する英雄物語です。四十七士の主君・浅野内匠頭（あさのたくみのかみ）は、上役の吉良上野介（きらこうずけのすけ）からの度重なる侮辱に耐え切れず、江戸城で刃傷沙汰を起こしたことにより切腹を命じられました。一方の吉良上野介はお咎めなしだったことから、主君の無念を晴らすため、四十七士は入念な仇討ち計画を立てて、ついに宿敵の屋敷に潜入。吉良を斬り殺し、無念を晴らしたのでした。敵の首を主君の墓に捧げたあと、彼らはそろって自首しました。主君の名誉を守った仇討ちは人々の共感を呼び、彼らの生きざまは伝説として語り継がれています。

山科義士まつりでは、この義士隊に扮した山科区民の行列が、毘沙門堂から大石神社まで山科一帯を練り歩きます。道中では東映画村の俳優の指導のもと、区民と俳優が一緒になって、有名な「松の廊下」「浅野内匠頭の切腹」「討ち入り」のシーンを演じるなど、見ごたえもたっぷりです。この日は、山科のあらゆる年代の人々が参加し楽しむ日。日本人の心に生き続ける義士たちへの人々の強い思いが感じられる祭りです。

【山科義士まつり】開催日程／12月14日
京都市山科区一帯　10:00〜14:30ごろ　毘沙門堂〜外環状線〜東部文化会館〜岩屋寺〜大石神社
料金／無料　JR・地下鉄山科駅下車、徒歩20分（毘沙門堂）　地下鉄椥辻駅下車、徒歩30分（大石神社）
問い合わせ　☎075-592-3088　山科義士まつり実行委員会（山科区役所地域力推進室まちづくり推進担当）
【Yamashina Gishi Matsuri】DATE：December 14
Around Yamashina-ku, Kyoto City　10:00〜14:30　Bishamon-do〜Sotokanjō-sen〜Tōbu-bunkakaikan 〜Iwaya-dera〜Ōishi Jinja　Fee：Free　☎075-592-3088（Yamashina City Hall）
http://www.bishamon.or.jp/

義士会法要 法住寺

Gishi-e Hōyō | 47 Rōnin Memorial Service Hōjū-ji

本堂の隣には四十七士、上段に主君・浅野内匠頭の木像が安置されています。太夫道中を奉納した菊川太夫はとても美しい方でした。
There are wooden statues of the 47 Rōnin and their lord enshrined in the main hall's side room. The *tayū* who participated in the ceremony, Kikugawa Tayū, was most gracious.

 7,241 いいね！

The story of the 47 Rōnin is a classic tale said to embody the spirit of the samurai code of honor, in which forty seven retainers, left without a master when their lord was forced to commit suicide, plan for years before taking revenge against the man who slighted him. While the *rōnin* made their preparations, their leader, Ōishi Kuranosuke, resided in Kyoto, pretending he had lost his honor and spending his time in teahouses. It is said he made pilgrimage to Hōjū-ji to pray as well as to meet secretly with his comrades to plan their attack. As a result, Hōjū-ji holds a 47 Rōnin Memorial Service each year on December 14th, the anniversary of the night the *samurai* sacrificed their lives to clear their lord's honor.

The day's ceremonies start with a *tayū dōchū* procession. Once the *tayū* (courtesan) has entered the main hall, the religious portion of the festival, a memorial service, is conducted by the head priest of Hōjū-ji for the 47 Rōnin. The *tayū* performs a tea offering, and the interior is packed with people who wish to pay their respects. After the service concludes the temple hosts several rounds of tea ceremony presided over by a *maiko* (apprentice geisha) and the *tayū*. Visitors can also enjoy a tasty bowl of "night raid" soba outside the main hall.

四十七士の物語は「武士道」の魂を表しているといわれています。高家旗本に逆らったことにより主君は切腹させられ、赤穂藩の侍は浪人になりました。約2年の準備期間を経て、47人の浪士は仇の屋敷に討ち入り、主人の仇を討ちました。

筆頭家老で四十七士のリーダーであった大石内蔵助は、準備の2年間、敵を油断させるために京都のお茶屋で遊びほうける振りをしていました。その際、密かに法住寺を訪れて身代わり不動尊に祈りを捧げ、討ち入りの成功を願ったといわれていることから、法住寺では討ち入りが行われた12月14日に「義士会法要」が行われています。

この日の朝、大玄関前から竜宮門まで、島原の太夫による太夫道中が奉納されます。太夫は昔ながらの装束を身にまとい、お歯黒（おはぐろ）にして、禿（かむろ）という太夫に仕えるふたりの女の子を伴っています。太夫が本堂に入ってから、法住寺の住職が約1時間の法要を行ったあと、舞妓さんによる献茶が奉納され、たくさんの人々が参拝します。法要が終わってから舞妓と太夫がお点前するお茶会も行われます。このお茶会にも四十七士に関する内容が盛り込まれており、四十七士のひとり・原惣右衛門が討ち入り前に書いた手紙の掛け軸が飾られます。肌寒い冬の一日、参拝者には、おいしい討ち入りそばも振る舞われます。

【法住寺】開催日程／12月14日
京都市東山区三十三間堂廻り町 655　☎ 075-561-4137　10:30 〜　料金／無料
【Hōjū-ji】DATE：December 14
655, Sanjūsangendō Mawari-chō, Higashiyama-ku, Kyoto City
☎ 075-561-4137 10:30 Fee：Free
http://hojyuji.jp

御煤払い 西本願寺
Osusuharai | New Year's Cleaning　　Nishi Hongan-ji

12月20日、早朝から始まります。参加者は北海道など遠方からも多く訪れています。
The event starts very early in the morning. People travel from as far away as Hokkaido.

今から私も家の大掃除をします！このお寺のように綺麗にはならないとは思いますが！（アメリカ）
I'm about to do a "year's worth of clean" myself on my house. I highly doubt it will be as good as the temple's though.

Though in the Western world it is more common to hear about "spring cleaning", the Japanese tend to do their annual home clean-up in winter— just before the New Year begins and most people return to their hometowns to spend time with their families. However, it isn't only family homes that need a good scrubbing during this period, but also offices, shops, and even Kyoto's many temples and shrines. Rather than doing it quietly themselves, one large temple in Kyoto has turned its "winter cleaning" into a giant community event.

Nishi Hongan-ji, a large Pure Land temple near Kyoto Station, hosts its Osusuharai in late December, and volunteers from the local area, as well as constituents from affiliated temples all over the country, come to participate. Clad in aprons and smocks with masks and towels wrapped around their faces to protect from dust, over 500 volunteers attended the Osusuharai last year. The volunteers work hard from early morning, beating the *tatami* mats, fanning dust out of the halls, and wiping the floors while the monks take to the rafters and ladders to dust the golden treasures and delicate wooden scrollwork. If you visit in the winter and want to play a part in helping preserve a historical temple, consider masking up for the Osusuharai.

「大掃除」というと、多くの人々がなかなか始められないことのひとつではないでしょうか。日本では一年を締めくくる大掃除が恒例行事となっており、東京の浅草寺（せんそうじ）や、大仏で有名な奈良の東大寺など、さまざまな寺社仏閣でも行われています。

親鸞聖人（しんらんしょうにん）を宗祖とする西本願寺の「御煤払い（おすすはらい）」は、室町のころ、蓮如上人（れんにょしょうにん）の時代から始まったといわれています。これは、一年を無事に過ごせた喜びと感謝を表しています。御影堂と阿弥陀堂にたまった1年間のほこりを払うため、僧侶や全国からの門信徒が参加。早朝7時よりマスクやタオルで完全防備した約500人が集まって、ほうき・雑巾・はたき・大うちわを手に掃除を開始します。とりわけ巨大な大うちわは、西本願寺の御煤払いの特徴として有名です。古式に習い、お寺全体がきれいになるまで、数百畳という広い室内を隅々まで掃除します。堂内では門信徒が横一列に並び、すす竹で畳をたたきながら進む様子が圧巻です。舞い上がったほこりは、大うちわで外に扇ぎ出していきます。

同日、東本願寺でも同じく「お煤払い」が行われます。

【西本願寺】開催日程／12月20日
京都市下京区堀川通花屋町下ル　☎ 075-371-5181　5:30 〜 17:00（季節によって異なる）
料金／無料（御煤払い参加・見学）
市バス西本願寺前下車すぐ
【Nishi Hongan-ji】DATE：December 20
Horikawa-dōri, Hanaya-chō-sagaru, Shimogyō-ku, Kyoto City　☎ 075-371-5181
5:30 〜 17:00（Changes seasonally）　Fee：Free（both viewing and participation）
http://www.hongwanji.or.jp/

世界一人気の神

伏見稲荷大社の千本鳥居　伏見稲荷大社

Senbondorii | Thousand Torii Gates　Fushimi Inari Taisha

伏見稲荷大社は長年、国内外を問わず初詣（新年の最初の神社参拝）の神社として日本屈指の人気を誇っています。
Fushimi Inari has been a popular spot for *hatsumōde* (the first Shintō shrine visit of the New Year) for many years.

こんな素敵な場所を見ていたら、
どんどん日本が好きになっちゃう。
Looking at these beautiful places,
I fall in love with Japan more and more.

Fushimi Inari is a popular tourist spot loved not only by the Japanese, but also tourists from around the world. Situated in southern Kyoto, Fushimi Inari is a shrine founded in the 8th century. There are over 30,000 Inari shrines in Japan, and Fushimi Inari Taisha serves as the headquarters of all of them. Particularly famous for its beautiful vermillion *torii* gates, it can feel like you're walking through a never-ending sea of red with over 10,000 gates (*senbondorii*) leading up Mt. Inari. The tradition of donating a *torii* gate if a wish is granted or to pray for prosperous business has been carried out for 200-300 years, resulting in the "thousand gates".

Fushimi Inari has been a popular spot for *hatsumōde* (the first Shinto shrine visit of the New Year) for many years. From January 1st to the 3rd, the shrine is filled with people who want to make their first wish, with an estimated 2.7 million visiting during that period.

伏見稲荷大社は、日本人だけではなく世界中から訪れる旅行者たちにも大人気の観光スポットです。1月1日から3日の間、境内は初詣の参拝者であふれ、西日本で最多の人が訪れるともいわれています。京都南部に位置し、創建は8世紀というたいへん古い神社です。日本全国に3万社以上の稲荷神社がありますが、古くから稲荷信仰の場として崇められてきた伏見稲荷大社は、その総本宮にあたります。

とりわけ稲荷山の参道に沿って奉納された「朱色の鳥居」は圧巻で、世界中の人々が魅了されています。全部で1万本以上の鳥居があり、歩くとまるで終わりのない赤い門の海を進んでいるような気分になります。これは、無事に願いが叶った崇敬者が神社に感謝の気持ちを込めて寄進したもの。200～300年前から始まったこの伝統が、結果として1万本もの鳥居が建てられるに至ったのです。

伏見稲荷大社では、参道に沿って稲荷山を登ります。ふたつの池を過ぎて進むうち、だんだんと現実を離れ、日本の民話に登場する精霊や生き物たちの神秘の世界へと入り込むような気分になることでしょう。「奥社奉拝所」のそばには「おもかる石」という不思議な名前の石があります。ここにある石灯籠の前で願いごとをし、石を持ち上げてみてください。持ち上げたときに感じる重さが予想より軽ければ願いごとが叶い、重ければ叶わないといわれています。

【伏見稲荷大社】
京都市伏見区深草薮之内町 68　☎ 075-641-7331
8:30 ～ 16:30　料金／無料　JR 稲荷駅下車すぐ。
市バス稲荷大社前下車、徒歩 7 分。京阪伏見稲荷駅下車、徒歩 5 分
【Fushimi Inari Taisha】
68 Fukakusa Yabunouchi-chō, Fushimi-ku, Kyoto City　☎ 075-641-7331
8:30 ～ 16:30　Fee：Free
http://inari.jp

十日ゑびす大祭 京都ゑびす神社

Tōka Ebisu | Festival for Business　　Kyoto Ebisu Jinja

江戸時代の町娘の衣装を着た女優さん。
8日と9日には「宝恵かご社参」が行われ、
女優さんはかごに乗りこみ太秦の映画村
から神社へ参拝します。
The actress is dressed as a "*machi musume*", an Edo Period town girl in long-sleeved kimono. On the 8th and 9th a *hōekago* procession makes its way down the street and in to the shrine.

面白そう！ 今度京都に行ったら
この神社に行ってみなくちゃ！（カナダ）
Looks so interesting ! We'll have to check that shrine out next time we go to Kyoto.

The first major festival of the new year, Tōka Ebisu, is held at Kyoto Ebisu Shrine over a five-day period from January 8th to the 12th. The enshrined god, Ebisu, is one of the Seven Lucky Gods and considered the god of fishermen and commerce, so the festival is based around Ebisu's birthday on the 10th- hence the name Tōka ("Tenth Day") Ebisu. Though the religious ceremonies are primarily performed within the main hall, numerous events occur each day as visitors flock to the small shrine to pray for success in their businesses.

A lively festival where locals and tourists alike mingle to pray, purchase lucky charms for the coming year, and enjoy the tasty festival food stalls, Tōka Ebisu has something for everyone. In front of a small altar a shrine maiden performs sacred *kagura* dances to bless branches of leafy green bamboo (*fukuzasa*) for parishioners to receive and other maidens are quite busy helping people select which lucky symbols they want to attach to the stalk. On certain days women in traditional clothing (one day actresses, one day *maiko*) arrive at the shrine to pass out the lucky bamboo. Depending on what day you participate, you can watch a variety of rituals, such as *mochi* making, a palanquin procession, and the presentation of a lucky fish.

新年を迎えて最初の有名な祭り「十日ゑびす大祭（通称初ゑびす）」は、1月8日から12日まで、京都ゑびす神社で行われます。ゑびす様は七福神のひとりで、漁と商売の神様。ゑびす様の誕生日が10日のため、「十日ゑびす」と呼ばれ親しまれています。参拝者は商売繁盛の願いを込めて、さまざまなお守りと縁起物を福笹につけます。縁起物はそれぞれの意味を持っています。たとえば、鯛はゑびす様のシンボルのひとつ。そして俵は福を運んでくれるもの、蔵は中に福を溜めるもの、神楽鈴は福を呼んでくれるものです。職場や自宅に飾るために、参拝者は福笹を持ち帰ります。

祭りの行事はほとんど本殿前で行われます。祇園の中にあり、それほど大きくない神社ですが、新年や商売繁盛を祈るために何千人もの参拝者が訪れます。十日ゑびすの歌が流れる境内で、地域の人と一緒に祈り、お守りと福笹を手に入れて、おいしい屋台に行くのも楽しみです。小さな祭壇の前では巫女さんが参拝者のために福笹と神楽を奉納しています。ほかの巫女さんたちは、福笹につける縁起物選びを手伝います。10日と11日には着物姿の美しい女性が、福笹を授与してくれます。ほかにも、餅つき神事、宝恵かご社参、招福まぐろ奉納など、毎日違う儀式を楽しめます。ちなみに京都ゑびす神社は、日本の三大ゑびす神社のひとつ。禅僧・栄西が中国からの帰国船で大嵐に襲われた際、ゑびす様に守られ、無事帰ることができました。そのため栄西は建仁寺建立の際、境内にゑびす様をお祀りしました。

【京都ゑびす神社】開催日程／1月8日〜12日
京都市東山区大和大路四条南　☎ 075-525-0005　1月8日 9:00 〜 23:00、
1月9日 9:00 〜 1月11日 24:00、1月12日 9:00 〜 22:00　料金／無料
京阪祇園四条下車、徒歩6分。市バス四条京阪前下車、徒歩6分
【Kyoto Ebisu Jinja】DATE：From January 8 to 12
Yamatoōji Shijō-minami, Higashiyama-ku, Kyoto City　☎ 075-525-0005
January 8th 9:00 〜 23:00、9th 9:00 〜 11th 24:00、12th 9:00 〜 22:00　Fee：Free
http://www.kyoto-ebisu.jp/tooka.html

武射神事　上賀茂神社

Musha Jinji | Archery Ritual　　Kamigamo Jinja

上賀茂神社は京都でも最古の神社のひとつ。
封建時代の武士は弓も修練しました。
Kamigamo Jinja is one of the oldest
shrines in Kyoto. Archery in Japan was one
of the disciplines practiced by samurai.

すごく参加したいです！（イスラエル）
I really want to participate!!!

In early January, the Musha Jinji archery ritual is held at Kamigamo Jinja in northern Kyoto. Though based on a much older tradition, this archery event has been practiced annually in its current form since 1935. Related to the many purification rituals held before and after the New Year begins, the Musha Jinji involves archers and priests dressed in traditional attire shooting arrows at a target 1.8 meters (5.9 ft.) wide. The target has the character for *oni* (ogre or demon) written on it, and so in shooting it they are metaphorically cleansing negative energy and praying for good fortune for the coming year.

Once they proceed to the shooting range from the shrine's main hall where a more private ritual takes place, two priests fire special *kabura-ya* whistling arrows at the oni target before men from the Ogasawara school of archery dressed in beautiful period silks line up to shoot their arrows one after another. As each person pulls the arrow back, the expressions on their face reflect the serious nature of this ritual purification by arrow, as well as the concentration and beauty of form inherent in Japanese martial arts. Though the ritual is a somber affair, the Musha Jinji is beautiful in its dedication.

京都の美しさの最たるものは、100年、数百年、あるいは1000年の長きにわたって守り継がれている都の伝統行事です。今もなお、京都に住む人々が敬意をもって、これら伝統を受け継いでいるのは素晴らしいこと。旅行者にとって、いにしえからの行事を時代を超えて再現している様子を目の当たりにできることが、大きな魅力となっています。

1月16日、午前11時。京都北部の上賀茂神社において「武射神事」が行われます。これは1935年から毎年1回、神職などが「狩衣（かりぎぬ）」という伝統衣装を身につけ、幅1.8mの的に向かって弓を射る行事です。古来、日本では、弓矢は単なる武器としてだけではなく、儀式や祭礼、呪術、魔よけなどの道具としても使われてきました。この行事では「鬼」と書かれた的を射ることで、邪気を払い、幸福な一年を祈願するのです。最初に射るのは神社の神職です。ふたりの神職が音の出る鏑矢（かぶらや）を、裏側に「鬼」と書かれた的に向かって放ちます。次に色とりどりの美しい装束を着た小笠原流の弓士が一列に並び次々に矢を放ちます。弓を引く手は小刻みに震え、表情は真剣です。人々が真摯に、また大きな努力を払って古い伝統を受け継いでいるのに感動します。

【上賀茂神社】開催日程／1月16日
京都市北区上賀茂本山339　☎ 075-781-0011　10:30 ～　料金／無料
市バス・京都バス上賀茂神社前下車すぐ
【Kamigamo Jinja】DATE：January 16
339 Kamigamo Motoyama, Kita-ku, Kyoto City　☎ 075-781-0011　10:30　Fee：Free
http://www.kamigamojinja.jp/event/sep.html
http://www.kamigamojinja.jp/english/index.html（English）

大的大会　三十三間堂

Ōmato Taikai │ Archery Competition　　Sanjūsangen-dō

Every January, Sanjūsangen-dō Temple celebrates Seijin no Hi (Coming of Age Day) with the Ōmato Taikai archery competition, an event where about 2,000 young people from all over the country participate. Most famously, the young ladies compete wearing colorful *hare-gi* kimono and *hakama*.

With origins tracing back to 1606 when a samurai shot 51 arrows across the length of the long temple hall, something that evolved into a famous archery competition called the Tōshiya, the current Ōmato Taikai involves shooting at targets about 60 meters away- a challenge well worth watching!

毎年1月、三十三間堂では成人の日を祝う「大的大会」が行われています。日本全国から集まった約2000人の参加者が60m離れた的に向かって矢を放ちます。この伝統行事は、1606年に弓の名手、浅岡平兵衛（あさおかへいべえ）が長い寺の本堂の端から端まで51本の矢を射通して見せたことで盛んになり、それは後に120mを射通す「通し矢」と呼ばれる競技に発展し、寺の行事として広く知られるようになりました。「通し矢」は現在行われていませんが、弓射の伝統は成人の日の行事として伝えられています。晴れ着姿で1列に並んで弓を引く女性たちの表情は真剣そのもの。強さと美しさ、それは彼女たちが立派な大人であることを証明する瞬間でもあります。

【三十三間堂】開催日程／1月中旬
京都市東山区三十三間堂廻町 657　☎ 075-561-0467　9:00 ～ 15:30
料金／当日のみ無料公開　市バス博物館三十三間堂前下車すぐ。京阪七条下車、徒歩7分
問い合わせ／☎ 075-692-3484（京都府弓道連盟）
【Sanjūsangen-dō】 DATE：Mid-January
657 Sanjūsangen-dō Mawari-chō, Higashiyama-ku, Kyoto City　☎ 075-561-0467
9:00 ～ 15:30　Fee：Free（Ōmato Taikai only）　http://www.sanjusangendo.jp

京都タワー
Kyoto Tower

Built in 1964, Kyoto Tower is located on the north side of Kyoto Station, on top of the Kyoto Tower Hotel. Thanks to beautification height restrictions on most other buildings, this tower is the tallest building in Kyoto at 131 meters high. Night or day, you can get a breathtaking 360-degree view of the whole city from the observation deck, making it a popular date spot.

京都駅に到着するとまず、高くそびえる灯台のような形の京都タワーが目に入ります。高さ131メートルの京都タワーが駅の北側の京都タワーホテル上に建てられたのは1964年のこと。いまや京都タワーは完全に街の景観の一部。京都のシンボル的な存在になっています。展望室からは、昼夜を問わず360度市街を一望でき、人気のデートスポットにもなっています。運がよければ人気マスコットの「たわわちゃん」にも会えるかも。タワービル内には、土産店やレストランがあり、日本料理やお酒を楽しむこともできます。そしてなんと地下3階には大浴場があるのです。絶景を楽しんだあとは、ここで旅の疲れを癒しては？

【京都タワー】
京都市下京区東塩小路町 721-1 （烏丸通七条下ル）　☎ 075-361-3215
9:00 ～ 21:00　料金／展望室 770 円　JR 京都駅下車、中央口より徒歩 2 分
【Kyoto Tower】
721-1 Higashi-shiokōji-chō, Shimogyō-ku, Kyoto City　☎ 075-361-3215
9:00 ～ 21:00　Fee：770 yen（Observatory）
http://www.kyoto-tower.co.jp/kyototower/en/index.html

湯立神楽 城南宮
Yutate Kagura | Boiling Ritual Jōnan-gū

「湯立」とは伝統的な神道の儀式。日本各地の神社
で行われ、参列者は拝礼します。
Yutate is an ancient Shintō ceremony celebrated
all over Japan at different shrines.

京都の写真はいつ見ても
飽きません。（インドネシア）
Never tired seeing
moments of Kyoto.

Getting splattered by boiling hot water is not usually what you'd call a pleasant experience. But if you attend a Yutate Kagura ritual in Japan, you'll find people are actually trying to get a few drops of the sacred water on them in the hopes of receiving a blessing. This Boiling Ritual is common in Shintō, and Jōnangū Shrine in southern Kyoto holds its annual ceremony in January.

Starting off with a sacred kagura dance performed by four shrine maidens, the main event features a senior *miko* (shrine maiden) using bamboo leaves to scatter hot water from the *ōgama* pot on to spectators gathered around. It is believed that you can live free from disease, natural disasters, and bad luck if you are touched by this water. Each time the *miko* lifts her arms to bring the bamboo into the air she disappears into the steam for a few seconds, producing a very dramatic effect. This day also sees shrine maidens and priests performing blessings and cleansings for visitors who request them, and the bamboo itself is later available as a lucky symbol.

普通は、だれかにお湯をかけられることは気分のよいものとは言えないでしょう。しかし湯立神楽の儀式では、神聖な湯滴にふれることで、無病息災、願望成就が叶うとされています。この伝統的な神道の儀式は日本各地の神社で行われ、単に「湯立（ゆたて）」や、「湯神楽（ゆかぐら）」とも呼ばれています。

1月20日、京都市南部の城南宮で湯立神楽が行われます。儀式は、薪に火を点け、大釜に湯を沸かすところから始まります。神楽鈴や扇を手にした4人の巫女が祓神楽を舞い終えると、襷（たすき）掛けの巫女が「文政六年癸未二月」（1823年）の銘を持つ直径70cm近い大釜の前に進み出ます。「杓取の儀（しゃくとりのぎ）」では、巫女が柄杓で天の水をすくって大釜の沸き立つ湯に注ぎ入れる所作をし、塩を撒いて釜を清め、湯に洗米と酒を入れます。次に笛や太鼓の音に合わせ、御幣（ごへい ＊お祓いに用いる白紙を木の棒にとりつけたもの）を持って舞います。そして両手に持った笹の葉で勢いよく釜の湯を散らして邪気を祓い、無病息災、心願成就を祈ります。

巫女が笹を持った両手を振りかざすたびに、その姿がしばらく湯気の中に隠れる光景は迫力満点です。厳かな神事や巫女の舞踊も必見！儀式後には幸福の笹（有料）をいただくこともできます。

【城南宮】開催日程／1月20日
京都市伏見区中島鳥羽離宮町7　☎075-623-0846
地下鉄・近鉄竹田駅下車、徒歩15分。市バス城南宮東口下車、徒歩3分
【Jōnan-gū】DATE：January 20
7 Nakajima Tobarikyū-chō, Fushimi-ku, Kyoto City ☎075-623-0846
http://www.jonangu.com/newyear.htm

裸踊り　法界寺

Hadaka Odori | Naked Dance　Hōkai-ji

寺では1月に修正会（しゅしょうえ）といわれる
法要をします。法界寺ではこの修正会の最後の日
に裸踊りの行事が行われています。
Buddhist temples hold services called Shushō-e
in the new year, and the Hadaka Odori is the final
ceremony for Hōkai-ji.

👍 12,202 いいね!

宗教上の意味を持つ儀式は
素晴らしいですね！（ネパール）
Religious ceremony has its own
significance.

Like many temples, Hōkai-ji holds services throughout the New Year period until January 14th, a day called Kechigan-bi, when to celebrate the end of these observances the temple is host to a local event called the Hadaka Odori. With a history tracing back 200 years, this "Naked Dance" is dedicated to praying for an abundant harvest, the locals' happiness, and wish fulfillment. Very much a community affair, the participants are all locals, and their families turn out to enjoy the festival and provide warm soup to all.

The festival begins with priests proceeding to the Yakushi Hall, where sutras are read while young boys take to the stage of the Amidha Hall, replaced later by a group of adult men. Both groups stamp their feet and jostle each other, hands raised as they clap and chant *chōrai, chōrai*, an expression of utmost devotion to the Buddhas asking for their blessing. The men douse themselves in water from the well to purify their bodies before taking the stage, and the steam that rises off them is just a reminder of how cold they must be wearing only loincloths! After the dancing winds down the priests emerge and go around the Yakushi Hall blessing those assembled. For those looking for a glimpse into more local traditions, Hōkai-ji makes an interesting one!

京都の東南にある法界寺では、「裸踊り」と呼ばれる行事が1月14日に行われます。この裸踊りは、五穀豊穣、万民快楽と所願成就を祈るための修正会という法会の結願日（けちがんび）に行われ、江戸時代からの歴史ある祭礼で、地元の人々が参加します。とても寒い夜の行事では、参列者に粕汁が接待（※ふるまわれること）されます。

僧侶たちは薬師堂に入堂し、経を読み上げ、参列者は外で祈りを捧げます。裸踊りに参加するのは地元の小学生の男子と、青年・壮年の男性の2グループ。冷たい井戸水を全身にかぶり体を清めたあと、足踏みしながら手をあげて叩き「頂礼、頂礼」と大きな声を出しながら踊りを奉納します。撮影した日の気温は6℃とかなり寒く、体から上がった湯気から、寒さ厳しい冬の時期に裸で踊ることがいかに過酷な体験かが伝わってきます。僧侶たちは薬師堂から出て、縁側でお経を唱えながらまわり、集まった人たちの所願成就を祈ります。

法界寺は、藤原家の流れをくむ日野家が1051年に建立しました。薬師堂の中に祀られている薬師如来は「乳薬師」の異名を持ち、妊娠中の婦人が祈ると乳の出がよくなるそう。裸踊りも母性に繋がっており、踊りに使用した褌（ふんどし）を妊娠中の婦人の腹帯として使うと安産になる、といわれています。阿弥陀堂は1221年に焼失しましたが、すぐに再建され、中には国宝の阿弥陀如来が祀られています。

【法界寺】開催日程／1月14日
京都市伏見区日野西大道町19　☎075-571-0024　19:00〜21:00　料金／裸踊り無料、当日は一般拝観はなし
京阪バス石田下車徒歩13分。京阪バス日野薬師下車すぐ
【Hōkai-ji】DATE：January 14
19 Hino Nishidaidō-chō, Fushimi-ku, Kyoto City　☎075-571-0024　19:00〜21:00
Event Fee：Free
http://kanko.city.kyoto.lg.jp/detail.php?InforKindCode=1&ManageCode=1000206

節分

廬山寺、北野天満宮、八坂神社

Setsubun

Rozan-ji, Kitano Tenman-gū, Yasaka Jinja

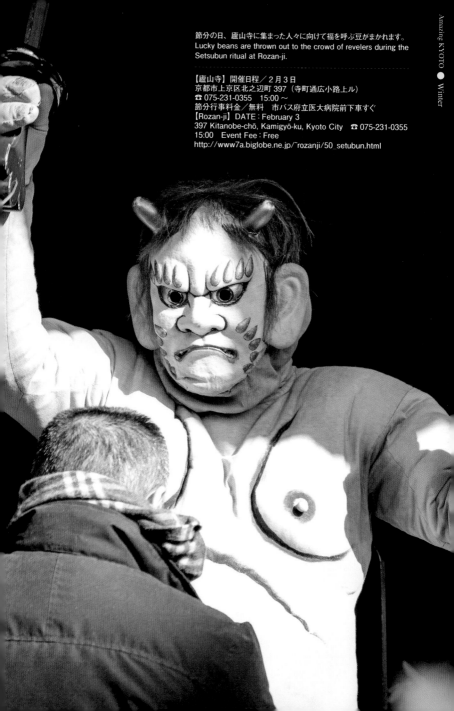

節分の日、廬山寺に集まった人々に向けて福を呼ぶ豆がまかれます。
Lucky beans are thrown out to the crowd of revelers during the
Setsubun ritual at Rozan-ji.

【廬山寺】開催日程／2月3日
京都市上京区北之辺町397（寺町通広小路上ル）
☎ 075-231-0355　15:00 〜
節分行事料金／無料　市バス府立医大病院前下車すぐ
【Rozan-ji】 DATE : February 3
397 Kitanobe-chō, Kamigyō-ku, Kyoto City　☎ 075-231-0355
15:00　Event Fee : Free
http://www7a.biglobe.ne.jp/~rozanji/50_setubun.html

写真上段は 2013 年の北野天満宮節分祭の様子。
写真下段は、八坂神社で舞楽と舞妓さんたちの
舞踊が披露されたものです。
The photo (above) is the from the 2013
Setsubun at Kitano Tenmangū. In Yasaka Jinja,
the groups performed traditional dances on
the stage (below).

僕も節分祭りに参加してみたいです！（イラク）
I wish I could attend the Setsubun
festival.

Japan celebrates Setsubun every year on February 3rd, the day before the beginning of spring according to the lunar calendar. This holiday is known for its *mamemaki* (bean throwing) tradition, where people throw roasted soy beans out the door of their homes or chase a family member wearing a demon mask shouting "oni wa soto" (demons out) and "fuku wa uchi" (good luck in) to invite fortune to their homes and chase out the bad. Celebrated not just at home, but as a community, Setsubun rituals can also be found at local shrines and temples all around Kyoto.

The Setsubun celebration at Kitano Tenmangū Shrine is famous for the *maiko* and *geiko* from the Kamishichiken district who throw packets of lucky soy beans into the excited crowd after performing traditional dances as offerings to the deities. Yasaka Shrine is also popular thanks to the lovely artists from Gion in attendance as well as other dances performed in traditional court style. In contrast to the lovely geisha, some places such as Rozan-ji Temple are known for its rather realistic *oni* demons. Some places host raffles and toss out lucky beans, some focus on the bad luck, and some on the good. No matter which shrine or temple you chose, celebrating Setsubun in Kyoto is an unforgettable experience.

季節の変わり目に祭りや儀式を行うのは、万国共通です。陰暦で春の訪れの前日にあたる節分には、悪霊を追い払い、来たる年に福を招く行事があります。この日、それぞれの家庭では豆まきが行われます。「鬼は外、福は内」と声をかけながら悪の象徴である「鬼」に向かって、炒った大豆を投げて災厄を祓います。

市内各所の寺社仏閣でも節分会が行われています。2月2日、祇園にある八坂神社の舞殿では、雅楽の演奏と舞楽という古典舞踊を見ることができます。雅楽とは、古代の宮廷音楽で中国から伝わったものですが、今なお中国のはるか昔の伝統を色濃く残しています。雅楽の演奏と舞楽が披露されたあと、宮川町の芸妓さん、舞妓さんが登場し、舞踊を奉納します。舞踊のあと、出演者たちが一同に舞台から豆まきを行います。

廬山寺の節分（82ページ）は一風変わった楽しい節分祭です。松明（たいまつ）と宝剣を持った赤鬼、大斧を持った青鬼、大槌を持った黒鬼が登場します。邪気払いされた三鬼は、逆に今度は人々の病気平癒、身体健全をはかるのです。北野天満宮での節分祭も、芸妓さん、舞妓さんが天神様に踊りを奉納したあと、見物客に向かって豆の入った小袋を投げてくれます。豆まきが始まると境内は歓喜にわきます。このように京都ではだれでも気軽に伝統芸能にふれて楽しめる祭事がたくさんあります。

【北野天満宮】開催日程／2月3日
京都市上京区馬喰町 ☎ 075-461-0005 10:00～ 料金／無料 市バス北野天満宮下車すぐ
【Kitano Tenman-gū】 DATE：February 3
Bakuro-chō, Kamigyō-ku, Kyoto City ☎075-461-0005 10:00 Fee：Free
http://kitanotenmangu.or.jp/

【八坂神社】開催日程／2月2日～3日
京都市東山区祇園町北側 625 ☎075-561-6155 9:00～ 料金／無料
市バス祇園下車すぐ。京阪祇園四条下車、徒歩5分
【Yasaka Jinja】 DATE：From February 2 to 3
625 Gion-machi-kitagawa, Higashiyama-ku, Kyoto City
☎ 075-561-6155 9:00 Fee：Free
http://www.yasaka-jinja.or.jp/event/setsubun.html

紀元祭　上賀茂神社
Kigen-sai | Foundation Day Festival　Kamigamo Jinja

武道では常に「心・技・体」の修練を重んじています。
精神面を大切にしている柊友会が剣道を奉納。
The kendō offering was performed by the Shūyūkai.
As with all Japanese martial arts, there is a focus on
the spiritual aspects of the art.

これを見るのが夢です！（アルジェリア）
Dreaming to see it!

On February 11th Japan celebrates National Foundation Day, commemorating the creation of the country of Japan and the ascension of the largely-mythical Emperor Jimmu, who was led to Yamato Province from Kumano by a divine three-legged crow, Yatagarasu. The *yatagarasu* is said to be related to the Kamo clan, and the Kamigamo Jinja, where ancient members of that clan are enshrined, now hosts the Kigen-sai ritual annually thanks to this connection.

Kamigamo Jinja's Kigen-sai is host to several sports-themed offerings starting with a *kendō* demonstration performed before the Hosodono Hall. Priests and athletes assemble before a flagpole on the precincts for a rendition of the national anthem, "Kimi ga Yo", and a flag raising. After that, a karate offering is performed while the priests conduct a ritual to pray for the peace of the country. The finale of the day is a game of *kemari*, a ball sport once played by Heian Period nobles.

For those interested in martial arts, the historical and rare treat of a *kemari* game, or the patriotic Kigen-sai rituals, take yourself to Kamigamo Shrine on February 11th.

日本の初代天皇・神武天皇（じんむてんのう）の即位の日といわれる2月11日は、建国記念の日とされています。神武天皇の御世は、紀元前660年からといわれ、神武天皇は八咫烏（やたがらす）の導きにより熊野から大和に移り、大和を都と定めました。上賀茂神社に伝わる神話では、八咫烏は678年に上賀茂神社を建立した賀茂氏の祖である賀茂建角身命（カモタケツヌミノミコト）の化身だといわれていることから、毎年この日に「紀元祭」を行っています。

上賀茂神社の紀元祭では、朝からさまざまな武道の奉納が行われます。初めに立砂がある細殿の前で剣道の奉納が行われます。そして神職の方々と参加者は旗の近くに集まり、「君が代」斉唱と国旗掲揚が行われます。空手の奉納も行われたあと、神職たちは国の平和のために祈りを捧げます。そして紀元祭のフィナーレは、かつて平安時代の貴族たちが楽しんだ蹴鞠（けまり）の再現です。蹴鞠の選手たちが入場し、円の形に並んで、腕や手を使わずに、鞠が地面に落ちないように蹴り合います。

武道、伝統的な珍しい蹴鞠、愛国心のある儀式に興味があれば、ぜひ2月11日に上賀茂神社を訪れてみてください。上賀茂神社は日本全国でも最も歴史が古い神社のひとつとしても有名で、5月には有名な葵祭が行われる場所でもあります。

【上賀茂神社】開催日程／2月11日
京都市北区上賀茂本山339　☎075-781-0011　9:00～11:50
料金／無料　市バス・京都バス上賀茂前下車すぐ
【Kamigamo Jinja】 DATE：February 11
339 Kamigamo Motoyama, Kita-ku, Kyoto City　☎075-781-0011　9:00～11:50　Fee：Free
http://www.kamigamojinja.jp/event/kigensai.html
http://www.kamigamojinja.jp/english/index.html （English）

Looking for a Bargain?
The Antique Market Shimai Tenjin

骨董市へ行こう！　終い天神　北野天満宮　Kitano Tenman-gū

The Tenjin-san fleamarket, held on the 25th of every month at Kitano Tenman-gū, is famous for its bargains and rare finds. The market's name comes from Tenjin, the god of knowledge and scholarship, and the date commemorates the passing of the man who became the deity. Though held every month, the markets in January (Hatsu Tenjin) and December (Shimai Tenjin) are the largest.

Offering everything from the traditional to the modern, shop for kimono, art, and antiques just as easily as household goods or current fashions. There are also handmade crafts as well as local produce and greenery for sale- not to mention the stalls selling street food you can enjoy while browsing!

京都で有名な神社のひとつ、北野天満宮では毎月25日は縁日（フリーマーケット）です。「天神さん」と呼ばれるこの縁日は、平日でも雨の日でも行われます。朝から夕方まで、何百もの露店が境内とその周辺に並び、伝統工芸品から日用品までさまざまなものが売られています。骨董から、ジュエリー、洋服、手づくりクラフトや地元の野菜などの食べ物、盆栽や植木もあり、食べ歩きながら買い物を楽しむことができます。値切ることはOK ですが、ほどほどに。縁日の名前は、学問の神様の「天神様」が由来。天神様は平安時代に生きた学者で政治家、菅原道真公（845 〜903）です。北野天満宮でのさまざまな儀式やイベントは、菅原道真公にまつわる日に行われ、縁日も菅原道真公の月命日の25日に行われます。とりわけ、12月は「終い天神」、1月は「初天神」として大きく開催されます。

自宅に能面を飾ってみてはいかが？
How about displaying a *nō* mask in your home?

手づくりの正月飾りも新年を迎える出番を待っています。
Handmade New Year's decorations are abundant at the December market.

露店で販売していた手づくりのかわいい羊の小物。干支のアイテムもいろいろあります。
Fitting for the season, many crafts feature the next year's zodiac animal.

手づくりの「トンボ玉」もひとつずつ買えます。
Many original craft items can be found for making your own projects.

忍者の武器はアンティークだけに少し高額でした。
Rare antiques such as ninja weaponry and art prints are available- for a price.

帯にはさんだたばこ入れや印籠などが落ちないよう紐の先に「根付」を結んでいました。
Despite their age, many items retain a beautiful, traditional look.

【北野天満宮】開催日程／終い天神／12月25日、天神さん／毎月25日
京都市上京区馬喰町　☎075-461-0005　市バス北野天満宮下車すぐ
【Kitano Tenman-gū】 DATE：Shimai Tenjin・December 25, Tenjin-san・the 25th of every month
Bakuro-chō, Kamigyō-ku, Kyoto City　☎075-461-0005
http://kitanotenmangu.or.jp/

春

Amazing
KYOTO
Spring

桜で有名な春の京都は、
季節の移り変わりとともに
嬉しいときめきも運んでくれます

Famous for its cherry blossoms,
Kyoto in spring is a city
overtaken with joy in the
changing of the seasons and all
that entails.

京都の北・原谷にあるプライベートガーデン
原谷苑は、知る人ぞ知る桜の花園。春の桜
のシーズンは、ピンクと白の花々で囲まれた
小径が美しく、まるで天国へ通じる道のようで
す。苑内をゆっくり散策するには 20 ～ 40 分
ほどかかります。歩いていると、妖精にでも
出会えそうな雰囲気。
Haradani-en, a private garden hidden in
the northern foothills, transforms in to a
sakura paradise every spring, with
footpaths that wind through clouds of
pink and white petals.

- -

【原谷苑】日程／春（桜・梅）、秋（紅葉）
京都市北区大北山原谷乾町 36
☎ 075-461-2924
9:00 ～ 17:00　料金／有料（変動あり）
地下鉄北大路駅または JR 円町駅よりタク
シーで約10分。駐車場なし
【Haradani-en】 DATE：Spring, Autumn
36 Haradani Inui-chō, Ōkitayama,
Kita-ku, Kyoto City ☎ 075-461-2924
9:00 ～ 17:00　Fee：Varies
http://www.haradanien.com/

桜散歩 祇園白川／仁和寺／二条城
Cherry Blossom Viewing Gion Shirakawa, Ninna-ji, Nijo-jo Castle

祇園白川や哲学の道など、京都で花見のそぞろ歩きをすれば、あらゆる種類の桜を楽しめます。写真上／仁和寺　下左／円山公園　下右／二条城
In Kyoto you can see many types of cherry blossoms. It is said that there over 1000 varieties of *sakura* in Kyoto.

 **13,091** いいね!

桜って素敵！そこに彼氏と行きたいです！
（カンボジア）
Amazing sakura! I wish I could be there with my darling!

From gorgeous scenes of cherry blossoms set against the glowing dawn sky to the sight of flowers illuminated against the dark of night, whether they adorn a temple garden or simply stand beside a local home, the *sakura* of Kyoto are gorgeous in every aspect. The low *omurozakura* reach for the sky, while the long branches of weeping *shidarezakura* brush the ground. With colors usually ranging from pure white to bright pink, green-tinted *sakura* can also be found, as well as *yaezakura*, flowers with multi-layered petals fluffier than the standard five-petal variety. In late March and early May, wherever you go becomes a photo opportunity, with ethereal clouds of blossoms swaying gently in the breeze, petals dancing on the wind. Kyoto in *sakura* season is just as romantic as you've always imagined.

春といえば、まず思いつくのが桜。京都はなんと言っても桜の名所の宝庫です。さまざまなスポットで、それぞれ違った魅力を持つ桜の風景が楽しめます。毎年、3月の終わりごろから早咲きの桜が咲き始め、遅咲きで知られる仁和寺の「御室の桜」（おむろのさくら）は4月半ば過ぎころまで愛でることができます。

日本の桜は数えきれないほど多くの品種があり、花の色ひとつをとっても、濃いピンク色から純白のもの、珍しいところでは緑色のものまであります。花びらも一重咲きから八重咲きまであり、じつに豊かな表情を見せてくれます。特に天を突くような高さを誇る大木の桜や、反対に地面まで届きそうなほど枝を垂れる「しだれ桜」で知られる名所は、桜の時期には多くの観光客で賑わいます。どんな種類であっても、誰もが美しいと感じるのが桜の魅力ではないでしょうか。

夜にライトアップされるしだれ桜が独特の風情を醸し出す「祇園」や「白川」、あるいは「哲学の道」などのそぞろ歩きは、京都らしい情緒が感じられる散策コースです。二条城ではお城と桜のコラボレーションが楽しめます。いろいろな桜の名所を巡り、春にしか出会えない感動を味わってください。

【祇園白川宵桜ライトアップ】
開催日程／3月下旬〜4月上旬
京都市東山区元吉町　祇園白川
（川端通〜巽橋）
18:00 〜 22:00　料金／無料
京阪電鉄祇園四条駅下車、徒歩5分
【The Gion Shirakawa-Yoizakura Illumination】 DATE：
From late March to early April
Motoyoshi-chō, Higashiyama-ku, Kyoto City
18:00 〜 22:00　Fee：Free
http://www.gion-nawate.com/sakura/（京都祇園縄手繁栄会）

【仁和寺】
京都市右京区御室大内 33
☎ 075-461-1155
9:00 〜 17:00　料金／ 500 円
京福電鉄御室仁和寺駅下車、徒歩 2 分。市バス御室仁和寺下車すぐ
【Ninna-ji】
33, Omuroōuchi, Ukyō-ku, Kyoto City
☎ 075-461-1155
9:00 〜 17:00　Fee：500 yen
http://www.ninnaji.or.jp/

【二条城】
京都市中京区二条城町 541 （二条通堀川西入ル）
☎ 075-841-0096
08:45 〜 16:00　料金／ 600 円
市バス二条城前駅下車すぐ。地下鉄二条城前駅下車すぐ
【Nijo-jo Castle】
541 Nijojo-chō, Nakagyō-ku, Kyoto City
☎ 075-841-0096
08:45 〜 16:00
Fee：600 yen
http://www.city.kyoto.jp/bunshi/nijojo/

ひいなまつり　市比賣神社

Hiina Matsuri | Girl's Day Festival　Ichihime Jinja

女雛と男雛に扮した「ひと雛」を見ると、衣装の素晴らしさがわかります。女雛は、ピンク色から濃いピンクを表現するために5枚もの着物を重ねて着ています。三人官女の舞も披露されます。
The "Emperor" and "Empress" of the *hitobina* human doll set stand and show off their completed wardrobes.

この綺麗な写真は、何度見ても飽きません。ありがとう！
I never get tired of your beautiful photos! Thank you!

Occupying a modest courtyard between residential buildings just off Kyoto's busy Kawaramachi Street, you might not guess that Ichihime Shrine is actually one of the foremost shrines for women in all of Kyoto. With its strong connection to women, it's no surprise that Ichihime Shrine is host to one of the largest Girl's Day festivals in Kyoto!

A ticket good for entry to all the various activities hosted at the Hito·Machi Kōryūkan costs 1,000 yen and comes with a special spring charm. On one floor you can experience the sorts of games girls in ancient Japan played, as well as participate in a tea ceremony. There is a "living doll set" in the large community hall, with a dressing demonstration of the clothing worn by the Emperor and Empress presented step-by-step. Once the rulers are ready, the whole set is assembled with three court ladies and five musicians. After the Amagatsu Ritual is performed, the musicians play *gagaku* music in accompaniment to the "Kanjō no Mai" dance performed by the court ladies holding peach blossom branches.

For those with daughters, interest in the holiday, or a fascination with traditional Japanese clothing, be sure not to miss Ichihime Shrine's Hiina Matsuri!

ビルに囲まれた市街地の中に、市比賣神社はあります。小さな神社ですが、女神様だけを祀り、良縁、子授け、安産など女性に関するご利益があるとして人気です。なかでも「ひいなまつり」は有名です。女の子の健やかな成長を願い、日本では3月3日に全国でひな祭りが行われます。女の子がいる家庭では、階段状の棚に「ひな人形」を飾りますが、そのスタイルは地域によって異なります。

市比賣神社の「ひいなまつり」は、神社の境内だけでなく、向かいにある「ひと・まち交流館」でも開催され、ここでは神社関係者が束帯と十二単姿に扮した珍しい「ひと雛」も見ることができます。平安時代の女の子の遊びを体験したり、お茶席にも参加できるほか、大ホールで「ひと雛」の女雛と男雛の着付実演を見ながら西陣和装学院の学院長の説明を聞くこともできます。着付けを終えた女雛、男雛、三人官女、五人囃子がステージにそろうと、「天児の儀（あまがつのぎ）」が行われ、続いて五人囃子が演奏する雅楽のもと、桃の枝を持つ官女たちによる「官女の舞」が舞われます。

このイベントへの参加料は1000円で、桃と柳でつくられた特別なお守りもいただけます。ひな祭りや和装に興味がある人はぜひ参加してみてください。

【市比賣神社】開催日程／3月3日
京都市下京区河原町五条下ル一筋目西入ル　☎ 075-361-2775
9:00 ～ 17:00　料金／1,000 円　京阪電鉄五条駅下車、徒歩 5 分。市バス河原町五条下車、正面 3 分
【Ichihime Jinja】 DATE：March 3
Kawaramachi Gojō-sagaru Hitosujime-nishi-iru, Shimogyō-ku, Kyoto City　☎ 075-361-2775
9:00 ～ 17:00　Fee：1,000 yen
http://ichihime.net/schedule.html

流し雛 下鴨神社

Nagashibina

Girl's Day Festival　Shimogamo Jinja

「流し雛」の儀式は、人形を御手洗川に流すことで心を清め、厄を逃れられるといわれます。写真は儀式に参加した宮川町の舞妓さん。
Geisha apprentices pray as they let sacred dolls float downstream at the Nagashibina ritual on Girl's Day.

流し雛は平安時代に始まったといわれています。儀式の多い下鴨神社ですが、その多くは水に関係している儀式で、神職が神事でお祈りします。
The event is said to have started in the Heian Period. Many of the ceremonies held at the Shimogamo Shrine are related to water.

本当に素晴らしい！（チュニジア）
This is truly amazing!

March 3rd is Hina Matsuri (Girl's Day) in Japan, when families with young daughters traditionally display beautiful *hina* dolls in their homes filled with characters from ancient imperial court life. It is also common for public events to be held on this day to pray for a happy and healthy life for young girls, and one such ceremony in Kyoto is the Nagashibina ritual at Shimogamo Shrine.

For the Nagashibina, a couple dressed in Heian Period style clothing to represent the Emperor and Empress dolls of a *hina* set participate alongside other important community figures, geisha apprentices, and even local mascot characters in setting special straw doll figures in the sacred stream at the shrine, letting them flow away. Of course, any visitor can then do the same if they wish, taking the straw wreaths cradling the paper dolls in red kimono and setting them gently in the water. By letting these dolls float downstream, it's said that any bad luck intended for a girl will instead follow the effigy, keeping the real girl safe and healthy. This ritual is also accompanied by a cute chorus of schoolchildren. It's an interesting event to take in, whether you have a daughter yourself or not.

日本の女の子にとって、3月3日は特別な日です。女の子だけが特別にお祝いしてもらえるからです。女の子の幸せと健やかな成長を祈る日である「ひな祭り」ですが、その歴史は、災厄を祓うために人形（ひとがた）を身代わりにして川や海に流す習慣から始まりました。

この日を祝うため、日本のお寺や神社は特別な祭り（式典）を行います。京都にある下鴨神社では、「流し雛」と呼ばれるお祭りが行われます。下鴨神社は左京区に流れる賀茂川と高野川の間に位置します。下鴨神社は、世界遺産に登録されており、下鴨地域の重要な神社です。

この「流し雛」では、平安時代の衣装に身を包んだ男びなと女びなのふたりが、神社内を流れている御手洗川（みたらしがわ）にひな人形を流します。それに続いて、子どもたちや大人たちもひな人形を流します。このように人形を川に流すことで、災厄を祓い、幸せと健康を祈ることができるとされ、京都に春の訪れを感じさせてくれます。

【下鴨神社】開催日程／3月3日
京都市左京区下鴨泉川町　☎ 075-781-0010
10:00 〜　京阪電車出町柳駅下車、徒歩10分。市バス下鴨神社前下車、徒歩約5分
【Shimogamo Jinja】DATE：March 3
Shimogamo Izumigawa-chō, Sakyo-ku, Kyoto　☎ 075-781-0010　10:00
http://www.shimogamo-jinja.or.jp/saijik.html

東山花灯路　　東山周辺
Higashiyama Hanatouro | Illumination　　Higashiyama Area

美しくライトアップされた風情豊かな道を歩いて
いると、着物を着た人々にもたくさん出会います。
円山公園の池に映る眩い光も印象的です。
As you walk through traditional streets
illuminated by warm lights, you'll be surrounded
by people dressed in stylish kimono.

京都は最高の町です！
京都大好きです！（日本）
Kyoto is such a great city,
I love Kyoto！

From early to mid-March, the entire Higashiyama area in eastern Kyoto gears up for the fun-filled night event known as the Higashiyama Hanatouro. A chance for tourists to enjoy what Higashiyama has to offer after dark when temples and stores in this traditional area are usually closed, the Higashiyama Hanatouro was held this year from March 6th to March 15th. As it gets dark, the lights turn on from 6pm and stay on until 9:30pm, with lanterns lighting the paths all the way from historical Shōren-in Temple in northern Higashiyama to the world-famous Kiyomizu-dera Temple in southern Higashiyama. Not only do several shrines and temples offer special night admissions and illuminated gardens and buildings, but a lot of the event can be enjoyed for free simply by strolling through the area and enjoying art work created by local students, stunning living flower arrangements, and various performances.

Making the city of Kyoto into an even more romantic sight, the various traditional lanterns lining the paths of Higashiyama are sure to lead you through a lovely evening stroll! Check the Kyoto Hanatouro website for more information and watch for updates when next year's event rolls around so you can come and enjoy as well!

桜が咲き始める少し前の東山界隈は、今や恒例イベントとなった「東山花灯路」で賑わいます。毎年3月の中旬〜下旬、約10日間にわたって行われるこのイベントでは、ふだんは日暮れころにはクローズする寺院や神社をはじめ、周辺のショップなども夜までオープンし、ほのかな灯りがともされた道を散策しようと多くの観光客が訪れます。

あたりが暗くなる午後6時から午後9時30分まで、北は歴史深い青蓮院（しょうれんいん）から、南は世界的に人気が高い清水寺まで という広いエリアにおいて、散策路に路地行灯が並べられます。多くの寺院や神社、円山公園などでは、期間限定で夜間特別拝観とライトアップが実施されるほか、エリア内のさまざまなポイントで無料で楽しめる大学生のアート作品やいけばな作品の展示、パフォーマンスなども用意されています。寒さもやわらぎ、過ごしやすくなったこの時期、夜の京都をゆっくり楽しんでみてはいかがでしょう。

この人気ライトアップイベントの花灯路は、春の東山界隈のほか冬には嵯峨・嵐山界隈でも催されます。（p 58参照）

【東山周辺】開催日程／3月中旬〜10日間
京都市東山区下河原町八坂鳥居前下ル下河原町付近
18:00 〜 21:30　料金／散策無料（拝観料等別途必要）
京阪電車祇園四条駅・阪急電鉄河原町駅下車。市バス清水道・五条坂下車、徒歩約10分
問い合わせ／☎ 075-212-8173（京都・花灯路推進協議会事務局）
【Higashiyama Area】DATE : 10 days in March
Around Shimogawara-chō, Higashiyama-ku, Kyoto City
18:00 〜 21:30　Entrance Fee : Varies by Temple　☎ 075-212-8173（Comittee）
http://www.hanatouro.jp/index.html　http://www.hanatouro.jp/e/index.html（English）

青蓮院ライトアップ 青蓮院
Shōren-in Light-up | Illumination Shōren-in

青蓮院ではシンプルでありながら芸術性に富んだ
ライトアップを体験できます。円山公園では粟田
神社の有名な提灯が見られます。
Shōren-in temple's light-up is a beautiful, subtle
illumination. In Maruyama Park, Awata Shrine's
famous lantern floats are out to show their stuff!

結婚することになったら、
式は京都で挙げたいです。
If I ever get married,
it would have to be in Kyoto!

Illuminated at night during the Higashiyama Hanatouro period, Shōren-in's Shinden garden is covered in numerous small, blue spheres of light whose brightness ebbs and flows against the mounting darkness. Perching on the sanctuary steps, people are mesmerized by the soothing sight of the field of lights sparkling amidst the grass, and those walking through the garden paths stop to wonder for a while. After that magical sight it's hard to leave, but the inside of the temple is just as enjoyable. Tea and sweets are available in the Kacho-den, offering a view of a separate illuminated garden while guests enjoy their cup of green tea.

Following the pull of beckoning lanterns brings you to the amazingly crafted Awata Shrine lanterns, each one taking the shape of a famous legend or god. *Ikebana* displays are scattered across Maruyama Park as well as the path itself, and each one is striking. There is even a fox bride's procession through the streets! A single night isn't enough to see everything the Hanatouro has to offer, so you can be sure it will leave you wanting more!

Check the Kyoto Hanatouro website for more information and watch for updates when next year's event rolls around so you can come and enjoy as well!

紅葉の美しさで知られる青蓮院では、年に数回、一定期間のみ夜間拝観が行われており、「東山花灯路」と同時期に開催されています。そのときにほどこされる境内のライトアップは、よくあるイルミネーションとはまるで違います。夕闇の東山をバックに、青く輝く小さな光の玉が寝殿前の庭園一面に敷き詰められ、寝殿の階段に座りながら庭園を眺める人々はだれもがこれらに癒され、うっとりと魅了されています。庭園の中を巡っている人々も、ライトアップの前ではみな足を止め、感動の声をあげるはずです。その魔法のような光景を眺めていると、その場を離れるのが辛く感じられるほど。美しいお寺の内部も見学し、華頂殿に用意されたお茶席にも座って、青蓮院の魅力を堪能しましょう。

東山花灯路と同時期開催なので、青蓮院から行灯に沿って歩いていくと、神話や伝承をモチーフとした粟田神社の大燈呂や、円山公園の中と道沿いに展示された「いけばな作品」を見られたり、運がよければ散策中に「狐の嫁入り」行列にも出会えるかもしれません。とてもひと晩では時間が足りないほど、たくさんの見所にあふれています。詳細はp100〜101の東山花灯路の記事を見てください。

【青蓮院】開催日程／3月中旬〜10日間
京都市東山区粟田口三条坊町 69-1 ☎ 075-561-2345 18:00 〜 21:30
料金／800 円 市バス神宮道下車、3 分、地下鉄東西線東山駅下車、徒歩 5 分
【Shōren-in】DATE : 10 days in March
69-1 Awataguchi Sanjōbō-chō, Higashiyama-ku, Kyoto City ☎ 075-561-2345
18:00 〜 21:30 Fee : 800 yen
http://www.shorenin.com/night/ http://www.shorenin.com/english (English)

"はねず色"を身にまといます

はねず踊り　随心院
Hanezu Odori | Plum Festival　Zuishin-in

はねず踊りの伝統は一度途絶えましたが、1973年に地域の人々の努力により復活しました。
当日は今様踊りなど他の催しものも楽しめます。
The Hanezu Odori tradition had died out in the modern era until 1973 when the locals banded together to revive it.

すごく綺麗！ 本当に生で見てみたい。（ブルガリア）
So beautiful!
I really wish I could see it live.

Serving as a celebration of the coming spring season and in honor of the famous poet and beauty Ono no Komachi, Zuishin-in temple's Hanezu Odori is held each year on the last Sunday of March. Based on an old folk song and dance tradition, the Hanezu Odori tells the story of Ono no Komachi and her ill-fated would-be lover in The Tale of One Hundred Nights.

Four separate performances are scheduled throughout the day, with the Hanezu Odori performed first, followed by an Imayō dance. Local school girls practice dutifully after school to perform the charming Hanezu Odori, and the Zuishin Imayō is presented by two young ladies dressed in the style of *shirabyōshi*, female entertainers dressed in men's religious garb.

In addition to the Hanezu Odori dance performances, *mochi* rice cakes are pounded throughout the day, made ready to eat or take home, and special *uirō* candy, which is sucked out of bamboo tubes, is offered by the winners of the previous year's Zuishin-in Miss Ono no Komachi Contest. The Zuishin-in Plum Garden is also a lovely vision in pink. Wherever you look, you'll find plum blossoms, whether on the trees or tucked into dancers' hats or sashes. Anyone interested in traditional Japanese performances ought to take themselves to the next Hanezu Odori!

「はねず」とは、薄紅色のこと。小野小町ゆかりの寺院である随心院では、「はねず」と呼び親しまれている紅梅が咲くころ、毎年3月の最終日曜日に「はねず踊り」が行われます。美しい歌人といわれた小野小町と、彼女に恋した深草少将の物語である「百夜通い」が、山科区小野地域に昔から伝わる民謡をベースとした音楽と舞によって表現されるものです。踊り手は地域の子供たち。はねず踊りの踊り子は、季節のシンボルとして梅の枝を持っています。もの悲しい物語ではありますが、紅梅のような可憐な着物に梅の花をあしらった姿で、琴の伴奏と歌声が流れるなかで舞うこの踊りに、春を迎える人々の喜びが感じられるようです。

踊りは一日に4回行われ、「はねず踊り」とともに、平安時代の身分の高い女性が男性の装束を着て踊っていたという「今様踊り」も披露されます。白拍子（しらびょうし）の装束を着た今様の踊り子は、刀と梅の枝と舞扇を持っています。ほかにも、毎年ゲストが呼ばれて踊りを披露したり、「はねず踊り保存会」による餅つきの餅を味わうこともできます。ミス小野小町コンテストで選出された女性が販売する、竹の筒に入った「はねずういろう」もおみやげに人気です。鑑賞は有料ですが、このチケットで境内にある梅園にも入園できるので、春の随心院を存分に味わえることでしょう。

【随心院】開催日程／3月最終日曜日
京都市山科区小野御霊町35　☎075-571-0025
9:00 〜 16:30（踊りは11:00 〜、12:30 〜、13:30 〜、15:00 〜）　料金／1000 円
京阪バス小野下車、徒歩 1 分。地下鉄東西線小野駅下車、徒歩 5 分
【Zuishin-in】DATE：Last Sunday of March
35 Ono Goryō-chō, Yamashina-ku, Kyoto City　☎075-571-0025
9:00 〜 16:30（The Hanezu Odori 11:00、12:30、13:30、15:00）　Fee：1,000 yen
http://kyoto-design.jp/event/12207

大原女まつり 大原女の小径

Ōhara-me Matsuri | Women of Ōhara Festival　　Ōhara

大原は緑あふれる閑静な里。大原女まつりの時期でなくても、地元の観光業者が「大原女装束」を貸してくれるので、大原女になった気分を味わえます。

Even if you miss the festival itself, the local tourism agency allows visitors to rent the costumes and try them on for themselves.

京都を訪れたとき、
大原がいちばん気に入りました！（カナダ）
Ohara was my favorite place to visit when I went to Kyoto!

Ōhara is a small village with big rustic charm located on the north side of Kyoto, famous for its six historic Buddhist temples. Beyond its religious sites, the other iconic image of Ōhara is actually the Ōhara-me.

In the past Ōhara-me, "women of Ōhara", donned traditional farming attire of modified indigo kimono with red sashes and white headscarves to make their way several hours on foot into Kyoto proper, carrying flowers, produce, or firewood on their heads to sell in the city. Their uniform is said to be the sort of clothing worn by an attendant to Kenreimon-in, a tragic noblewoman in Japanese history who spent her later years secluded in Ōhara as a nun. Though Kenreimon-in passed in 1213, the Ōhara-me could still be seen selling their wares in distinctive costume up until a few decades ago.

The Ōhara-me Festival in May celebrates these proud Ōhara-me women with a large procession around the village made up of women and girls dressed the part. A two kilometer walk takes the group around the countryside scenery and past ancient temples, creating the impression you've slipped back in to the past for a moment as you watch. If you can't attend this day, the local tourism bureau rents Ōhara-me costumes for free if you'd like to wear one around town!

市内中心部から車で北へ1時間ほど。静かな山間部に、大原と呼ばれる集落があります。ここにはいくつかの有名な寺院、三千院、勝林院、寂光院などがあります。とりわけその代表格である三千院や平家ゆかりの寂光院は、観光スポットとしてもよく知られています。しかし大原の魅力はそれだけではありません。美しい「大原女」(おはらめ ＊おおはらめとも呼ぶ)のイメージが、この地域をより魅力的なものにしているのです。

その昔、大原の女性(大原女)は伝統的な野良着を着て、頭に花や農作物、薪などを載せ、数時間かけて京都の町まで歩いて行商に行きました。晩年を大原に隠棲した建礼門院の悲しい物語とともに、数百年に及ぶ大原女の暮らしも長く語り継がれています。

4月下旬～5月上旬には、この大原女を讃える「大原女まつり」が開催されます。なかでも注目したい行事が4月末の週末に行われる「時代行列」です。女性たちが、時代によって変遷してきたそれぞれの大原女装束を着て、寂光院から勝林院まで、この地域の周辺約2kmを行列して歩きます。事前に申し込めば、衣装を借りて行列に参加することもできます。歴史ロマンあふれる寺院巡りとあわせてあなたも一緒に歩いてみてはいかがでしょう。10月後半から11月にかけては「秋の大原女まつり」(勝林院出発、寂光院終点)もあります。

【大原女まつり】開催日程／4月下旬～5月上旬2週間
京都市左京区大原界隈
13:00 ～ 15:00 ごろ　料金／無料（入山料700円）　京都バス大原下車、徒歩10分
問い合わせ／☎075-744-2148（京都大原観光保勝会）
【Ōhara-me Matsuri】DATE：2 weeks, from April to May
Around Ōhara, Sakyō-ku, Kyoto City
Around 13:00 ～ 15:00　Fee：700 yen　☎075-744-2148（Association）
http://kyoto-ohara-kankouhosyoukai.net/

曲水の宴　城南宮
Kyokusui no Utage | Winding Stream Banquet　Jōnan-gū

日本の昔の貴族はさまざまに雅な遊びを楽しみました。歌人は歌題に合わせて和歌をつくり、短冊に書くと、童子が短冊を集めに回ります。出された和歌を神主たちが歌うように唱じ披露します。
Each poet chooses a poem to submit, which is later sung out by a chorus of shrine priests.

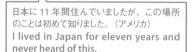 6,369 いいね！

日本に11年間住んでいましたが、この場所のことは初めて知りました。（アメリカ）
I lived in Japan for eleven years and never heard of this.

Kyokusui no Utage, an elegant form of leisure entertainment enjoyed by nobles in ancient Japan, is reenacted at Jōnan-gū Shrine in southern Kyoto twice a year in spring and autumn, with the spring "Wandering Stream Banquet" held on April 29th. Local poets dressed as Heian Period nobility in silk robes proceed into the garden and receive the year's theme from the shrine priests. This year the theme was "Yūgasumi", or "evening mist".

The ancient nobles were a cultured bunch. While being educated in poetry and composition was considered a sign of class, they also enjoyed the finer things in life- such as alcohol. *Sake* (rice wine) is poured into small cups and sent sailing down a small stream on bird-shaped boats, with little pages holding bamboo poles tending to the boats and assisting the poets, who enjoy an *imayō* dance performance before they set to writing to the sound of *koto* plucking in the background.

Set against a gorgeous garden in full bloom with iris, azalea, and wisteria, this ritual truly feels like a glimpse back in time to the sedate and ritualistic lifestyle of a Heian Period noble. If you're in Kyoto on April 29th or November 3rd, don't miss Jōnan-gū's recreation of the Kyokusui no Utage!

かつて、日本の貴族が楽しんだ歌遊びを今に伝える「曲水の宴」は、京都市の南エリアに位置する「城南宮」で一年に2回、春と秋に行われています。奈良時代（8世紀）から平安時代にかけて盛行したこの宴は、その後、武士の勢力が強まり行われなくなりましたが、城南宮で昭和時代に再現されました。城南宮では毎年4月29日と11月3日の14時から行われています。平安時代の貴族の装束を身に着けた歌人たちが庭に腰を下ろし、その日の歌題に合わせて和歌をつくります。

貴族たちは特別な趣向で宴を楽しみました。ゆるやかに庭園を流れる曲がりくねった小川のほとりで宴を催したことから「曲水の宴」といいます。そしてお酒を小さな器に入れて、鳥の姿をした舟（盃台）にのせ小川に流し、琴の音が流れる風情たっぷりな雰囲気の中で和歌をつくり短冊に書きます。座の横には、書のための小さな硯箱と、飲み干した盃に入れるための印として季節の草花の数片が置いてあります。また城南宮では平安時代の末に流行した白拍子（しらびょうし）の舞を見ることができます。

春の曲水の宴では、菖蒲、ツツジ、藤の花が咲く美しい庭を背景にしながら曲水の宴が行われて、まさに平安時代へとタイムスリップしたかのようです。城南宮の庭の美しさとともに、優雅な世界に酔いしれてください。

【城南宮】開催日程／4月29日、11月3日
京都市伏見区中島鳥羽離宮町7　☎075-623-0846
14:00 ～　料金／無料　地下鉄・近鉄竹田駅下車、徒歩15分
【Jōnan-gū】DATE：April 29, November 3
7 Nakajima Tobarikyū-chō, Fushimi-ku, Kyoto City　☎075-623-0846
14:00　Fee：Free
http://www.jonangu.com/kyokusuinoutage.htm

駈馬神事 藤森神社

Kakeuma Shinji | Trick Riding Festival　　Fujinomori Jinja

新緑の鮮やかな神社で行う駈馬神事。写真上は「手綱潜り」。手には花笠を持っています。
There are currently seven tricks in the program, all of which are related to traditional military maneuvers.

ワァー！ これすごーく
マジカルです！（オーストラリア）
Wow this is soooooooooooo magical.

Horses once played a big part in Japanese military endeavors as the samurai warrior class rose and fell from power. But these days, there aren't many chances to see horses up close in Japan. Still, in homage to their role on the battlefield, one shrine in southern Kyoto, Fujinomori Shrine, performs a traditional trick riding ritual each year. The current program includes seven different tricks said to be based on riding moves warriors would employ to avoid arrows, conceal themselves from enemies, and gather information.

Every year in early May, the *kakeuma shinji* (trick riding ritual) is held during the Fujinomori Festival. The gods of Fujinomori are known for their dominion over military prowess and victory, which is why warrior-inspired horsemanship is used as an offering for their entertainment. Of course, the many people who gather to watch the event enjoy it as well! Riders, called *noriko*, range from local men who are the latest in a generations-long tradition to men from other prefectures who become involved by hearing about the event. What they share is their passion for riding and preservation of this unique tradition.

息をのむ観衆、近づいてくる蹄の音、技を成功させた乗子への歓声…。藤森神社で行われる駈馬神事は、緊迫感と興奮に満ちた年に1度の行事です。

毎年5月5日、「藤森祭」の行事のひとつとして行われるこの神事は、そもそも武士たちの戦場での無事と勝利を祈って神に奉納されていたもの。昔の武士たちは刀や弓に加え馬術の訓練も積み、戦場で役に立つ創造的な乗り方や技法を編み出していきました。このダイナミックな神事を今も継承しているのは、もはや藤森神社のみです。駈馬神事では、敵矢が降りしきるなかを〝駈ける〟技「手綱潜り（たづなくぐり）」をはじめ、後ろにいる敵の動静を見ながら走る「逆乗り」、敵矢が当たったと見せかける技「藤下がり」、前線より後方へ情報を送りながら〝駈ける〟技「一字書き」、敵矢を打ち払いながら駈ける「矢払い」、敵に姿を隠す「横乗り」などの技が披露されます。

藤森神社の歴史は古く、平安遷都の前から存在していたといわれています。「菖蒲（しょうぶ）の節句」発祥の地ともいわれ、「菖蒲」は「勝負」に通じることから、勝運と馬の神社として今も信仰を集めているのです。この命がけのパフォーマンス、ぜひ間近で見ておきたいものですね。

敵をあざ笑う技「杉立」!

【藤森神社】開催日程／5月5日
京都市伏見区深草鳥居崎町 609 ☎075-641-1045
13:00 ～ 14:00、15:00 ～ 16:00 料金／無料
京阪電車墨染駅下車、徒歩 5 分。市バス藤森神社前、JR藤森駅下車、徒歩 5 分
【Fujinomori Jinja】 DATE：May 5
609 Fukakusa Toriizaki-chō, Fushimi-ku, Kyoto City ☎075-641-1045
13:00 ～ 14:00、15:00 ～ 16:00 Fee：Free
http://www.fujinomorijinjya.or.jp/kakeumasinnjinew2.html

小鬼、大鬼が踊ります

やすらい祭　今宮神社
Yasurai Matsuri | Festival for Sound Health　Imamiya Jinja

踊りの各組に子どもがふたりいます。この子は「神子」と呼ばれ、年齢に合った地域の男の子から選ばれています。花傘に見立てて設えた奉納所もあります。

Each group of dancers is accompanied by two page boys. These pages are called *kanko* (sacred children) and are chosen from the local boys.

装束が最高です！（女性）
The costumes are fantastic!

Heralded as one of Kyoto's three mysterious festivals, the Yasurai Matsuri at Imamiya Shrine is held each year in the middle of April to pray for good health and prevention of illness. Imamiya Shrine enshrines a deity of health and long life, but it is said that during the cherry blossom season he leaves the shrine to play tricks and becomes a god of sickness. In order to soothe his spirit, this lively festival features bright umbrellas decorated with flowers to lure the god back home.

Performers dressed as *oni* lead processions around the shrine grounds and perform three drumming dances to delight the deities. Young boys dressed as sacred pages carry small drums, and the accompanying group plays the flute, reads out a chant, and carries ritual weaponry. The red umbrellas are thought to bring good health for a year to those who pass under them, so it's not uncommon to see people lining up to wait for the chance to try to pass under one of these lucky umbrellas. For those praying for their health, effigies are also available for purification.

Watching this festival definitely left us with a mysterious feeling. If you're around in April, be sure to take a look for yourself!

京の三奇祭のひとつとして知られる今宮神社の「やすらい祭」は、疫病を鎮め、健康を願うために毎年4月第2日曜日に行われます。「練り衆」は12時に今宮神社の近くのお寺「光念寺」を出発し、町々を練り歩き、15時に今宮神社に到着します。

今宮神社に祀られている神様の御神徳は健康長寿です。昔から、桜の花が散るころ、疫神が花の精にあおられていたずらをしてまわり、それが疫病の源になるとされていました。疫神はやすらい踊りによって、たくさんの生花で飾られた大きな赤い花傘へと引き寄せられ、疫社へと鎮められることにより一年の無病息災を祈ります。練り衆からは「やすらいはなや」という声が時々聞こえてきます。そのやすらい祭が奇祭と呼ばれるゆえんは、赤と白のめでたい色の「鬼」の衣装を着た子供たちが独特な踊りを奉納するからかもしれません。鬼は、激しく飛び跳ねながら鉦（かね）や太鼓を叩いて踊ります。鉦や太鼓を打ちながら踊ることで、疫神を花傘へと引き寄せるのです。また花傘の下に入ると一年を無病息災でいられるといわれているので、訪れた際はぜひ花傘に入ってみましょう。ただし、多くの人が傘に入ろうと行列をつくっていますが…。

今宮神社で神事を斎行し、やすらい踊りを奉納したあと（約1時間）、光念寺に練り衆が戻り、やすらい祭は終了となります。ぜひこれらの鬼たちの踊りを、その目で確かめてください。

【今宮神社】開催日程／4月第2日曜日
京都市北区紫野今宮町21　☎ 075-491-0082
12:00 ～ 17:00　料金／無料　市バス今宮神社前下車すぐ
【Imamiya Jinja】 DATE : 2nd Sunday of April
21 Murasakino Imamiya-chō, Kita-ku, Kyoto City　☎ 075-491-0082
12:00 ～ 17:00　Fee : Free
http://imamiyajinja.org

春の花・キリシマツツジ　　長岡天満宮
Kirishima Tsutsuji | Azalea Garden　　Nagaoka Tenman-gū

長岡天満宮のキリシマツツジは高さ 2.5m を
超え、樹齢は 150 年以上と推定されています。
The Kirishima Azalea can grow over 2.5
meters, (8 ft.), in height, and are thought to
be over 150 years old!

👍 **11,911** いいね!

綺麗ですね !!!（ラオス）
Kirei desu ne !!!

Once the cherry blossoms have bloomed in Kyoto, the next flowers to open up are the numerous azalea bushes around the city. There are many different species of azalea, each with different colors and attributes, but some are especially noteworthy. One of these types is the Kirishima Azalea, a breed known for its unbelievably bright red color.

Nagaoka Tenman-gū, a lovely waterside shrine to the southwest of Kyoto city proper, is especially popular when the Kirishima Azalea begins to flower. With stone paths flanked by towering crimson azalea and beautiful views of the flowers along the nearby Hachijōgaike Pond, you'll feel like you've gotten lost in a sea of red clouds.

Though it can change slightly depending on the year and the weather, Kirishima Azalea usually start to bloom at the end of April, with Nagaoka Tenman-gū's azalea peaking on time this year in the last week of April. Once spring arrives in Kyoto, it isn't only the cherry blossoms that are worth getting out to see!

京都の桜が終わると、次にあちこちで咲き始める花がツツジです。ツツジにはさまざまな色や特徴を持つ種類がありますが、とりわけ美しいといわれる種類のひとつが、真紅の花を咲かせるキリシマツツジです。

京都市の南西に位置する、菅原道真公ゆかりの長岡天満宮は、キリシマツツジの名所として知られています。八条ヶ池のほとりの建物が昔の京都の雰囲気を醸し出し、「八条ヶ池ふれあい回遊の道」と名付けられた一帯は、真紅のツツジが道の両側を取り囲み、多くの人々に親しまれています。池のそばには少しだけ色が異なるツツジも植えられていて、見比べると、他のツツジとキリシマツツジの大きさや色の違いがわかります。鏡のように水面が輝く八条ヶ池とツツジの織りなす美しい景色に、きっと赤い雲の海に紛れ込んでしまったかのように感じるでしょう。

キリシマツツジは4月下旬に咲きますが、満開のタイミングはその年の気候に大きく影響されます。開花情報をよくチェックして、真紅に染まった長岡天満宮の境内をゆっくり散策してください。

【長岡天満宮】日程／見ごろは4月下旬（年によって異なる）
長岡京市天神 2-15-13　☎ 075-951-1025
9:00 ～ 18:00（4月～9月）、9:00 ～ 17:00（10月～3月）
阪急電鉄長岡天神駅西口下車、徒歩 10 分
【Nagaoka Tenman-gū】 DATE : Towards the end of April
2-15-13 Tenjin, Nagaokakyō City　☎ 075-951-1025
9:00 ～ 18:00（April ～ September）、9:00 ～ 17:00（October ～ March）
http://www.nagaokatenmangu.or.jp/keidai/keidai02.html

春の庭・勧修寺氷池園　勧修寺

Kajū-ji Hyōchi-en │ Garden in Spring　　Kajū-ji

四季を通してさまざまな花を見ることができます。春には花菖蒲やカキツバタが咲き誇ります。
The purple and yellow irises are particularly plentiful at Kajū-ji. The thin petals of the iris highlight its beauty.

 16,024 いいね！

平和的ですね！（アメリカ）
Peaceful!

It's said that April showers bring May flowers, and in Kyoto that expression certainly holds true! One of the many famous flowers that begins to bloom in May is the iris. A beautiful flower that has been popular in water gardens for centuries, there are three main types of iris in Japan, which come in a variety of colors and shapes.

In the water gardens of Kajū-ji, irises are particularly beautiful. This temple garden boasts several breeds of iris, as well as other lovely seasonal offerings such as water lilies and the later blooming lotus. Among the fresh green of spring, the contrasting purples, whites, and yellows offer a bright and colorful scene.

Because many different types of iris bloom at Kajū-ji, it's possible to see flowers in bloom from early May far into June, with concessions for weather and year. If you're lucky, you might also catch sight of a kingfisher or heron in flight between the flowers!

「4月の雨は5月の花を咲かせる」ということわざがありますが、この表現はまさに京都にぴったりです。5月に咲き始める花のひとつに、アイリス（英語名）があります。日本で代表的なアイリスは、「花菖蒲」「カキツバタ」「アヤメ」の3種類で、長きにわたり池泉エリアで愛されてきました。

これらアイリスが咲きそろうことで有名なのが、京都市の南部にある勧修寺。西暦900年の平安時代に醍醐天皇が創建したと伝わる由緒あるお寺です。勧修寺の観音堂には観音菩薩の像があります。またその昔、氷室池に張る氷を宮中に献上していました。その氷の厚さによって、その年の五穀の実りを占ったといわれています。この氷室池の水辺や中島には、5月中旬ころからカキツバタや花菖蒲が紫や白、黄色の花を目にも鮮やかに咲かせます。また水面には睡蓮の紅色が風に揺れ、訪れる人々の目を楽しませています。

春のこの季節、勧修寺ではこれら花菖蒲やカキツバタ、睡蓮などさまざまな花が楽しめるのと同時に、運がよければ、花のまわりを飛び回るサギやカワセミの姿も見つけることができるでしょう。

【勧修寺】日程／花菖蒲やカキツバタの見ごろは5月中旬〜下旬
京都市山科区勧修寺仁王堂町 27-6　☎ 075-571-0048
9:00〜16:00　料金／400円　地下鉄東西線小野駅下車、徒歩6分
【Kajū-ji】 DATE：From Mid-May
27-5 Niōdō-chō, Kanshū-ji, Yamashina-ku, Kyoto City　☎ 075-571-0048
9:00〜16:00　Fee：400 yen
https://kanko.city.kyoto.lg.jp/detail.php?InforKindCode=1&ManageCode=1000031

葵祭 京都御所〜下鴨神社〜上賀茂神社

Aoi Matsuri | Hollyhock Festival　　Kyoto Gosyo, Shimogamo Jinja, Kamigamo Jinja

葵祭行列の特徴のひとつは牛車。京都御所を出て、
町を通ってから下鴨神社の糺の森（ただすのもり）
へ向かいます。
The ox carts are one of the most original points
in the procession. They accompany the parade
from the Imperial Palace and head to
Shimogamo Shrine.

本当にすごく、すごく綺麗！
映画みたい！（ポーランド）
Just amazing - really, really beautiful -
looks like from a movie !!

Considered one of the three most important festivals in Kyoto, the Aoi Matsuri takes place on the 15th of May each year. Held by Kamigamo and Shimogamo Shrine, the origins of the festival can be traced all the way back to rites performed in the 6th century- and was established as a more formal annual event in the 9th century, when Kyoto became the capital and the Emperor recognized the importance of the Kamo shrines. Because of the *aoi* (hollyhock) leaves pinned to participants' hats, clothing, and carts, it earned the colloquial name of the Hollyhock Festival.

Various interesting ceremonies comprise the Aoi Matsuri, but the main event is the grand parade on the 15th. Starting from the site of the former Imperial Palace, hundreds of participants dressed in Heian Period clothing form two processions and make their way to Shimogamo Shrine and then on to Kamigamo, performing rites and making offerings at each. The Imperial Messenger's procession is first, accompanied by court nobles, soldiers, and offerings. The second, the Imperial Princess', is made up of noble women, ladies in waiting, and priestesses. A stately and aristocratic parade, watching the Aoi Matsuri go by creates the sensation of being transported back in time to the Heian capital.

京都の三大祭りのひとつとして知られている「葵祭」は、毎年5月15日に下鴨神社と上賀茂神社で行われます。葵祭の起源は6世紀、神様の怒りを鎮めて豊作を祈る儀式が始まりだと伝えられています。平安時代に京都が都となってから、この祭りは国家的な行事として執り行われるようになりました。「賀茂祭」という古くからの名称が「葵祭」になったのは、祭りの参加者の装束をはじめ、牛車（ぎっしゃ）までが葵の葉で飾られたからです。

葵祭の神事はさまざまありますが、最も大きな行事こそ、この行列にほかなりません。京都御所から始まり、何百人という平安時代の装束を身にまとった人々が前後ふたつの行列となって京都御所を出発し、下鴨神社と上賀茂神社で奉納と儀式を行います。

前の行列は勅使の列で卿相（けいしょう ＊三位以上の公卿）、兵士とともに神への供物が運ばれ、次の行列は斎王代（さいおうだい）の列で、命婦（みょうぶ）、女官、巫女がともに歩きます。斎王代に扮している女性は「およよ」という特別の乗り物で運ばれます。斎王代は毎年京都の由緒ある家庭の子女から選ばれています。大勢の見物客が見守るなか、当時の平安貴族を思わせる厳かな行列が通ると、そこはまるで平安時代にタイムスリップしたかのような雰囲気に包まれます。

【葵祭】開催日程／5月15日
10:30～京都御所／京都市上京区京都御苑3
11:40～下鴨神社／京都市左京区下鴨泉川町
15:30～上賀茂神社／京都市北区上賀茂本山339　問い合わせ／☎ 075-781-0010（下鴨神社）
【Aoi Matsuri】DATE：May 15
10:30 Kyoto Gosyo : 3 Kyoto Gyoen, Kamigyō-ku, Kyoto City
11:40 Shimogamo Jinja : Shimogamo Izumigawa-chō Sakyō-ku, Kyoto City
15:30 Kamigamo Jinja : 339 Kamigamo Motoyama, Kita-ku, Kyoto City
☎ 075-781-0010(Shimogamo Jinja)

春の庭・池泉庭園　神泉苑

Chisen-teien | Garden in Spring　　Shinsen-en

二条城を訪れるなら、小さくても見どころいっぱいのこの庭園にもぜひ立ち寄ってみてください。
When visiting Nijo-jo Castle make sure you don't miss this small but amazing garden! If you are planning to use the bus service while you are in Kyoto, look for the Shinsen-en-mae bus stop.

自然と建築の素敵なハーモニー！（イギリス）
Stunning harmony between nature & architecture!

Located on the south side of Nijo-jo Castle, the Shinsen-en ("Sacred Spring") Garden is one of the hidden jewels of Kyoto, where you can enjoy the charming characteristics of all four seasons, magnificent traditional architecture and beautiful Japanese landscaping all in one place.

Though it is now only 1/10th its original size, Shinsen-en is actually the oldest remaining garden in the city, originally built in the 8th century when Emperor Kanmu moved the capital and his palace to Kyoto. Once a sprawling 33 acres next to the Emperor's residence, the garden was reduced in size when Tokugawa Ieyasu became shogun in the early 1600's and used most of the land for his new castle, Nijo-jo. Now Shinsen-en is made up of a Shingon temple, a shrine to a rain goddess, a bridge famous for granting the wishes of those who cross it, and a boat with a dragon-shaped figurehead that doubles as a floating restaurant!

Boasting a variety of seasonal flowers, Shinsen-en is beautiful during camellia, cherry blossom, and azalea seasons, as well as in fall. If you visit Nijo-jo, make sure you don't miss this small but amazing garden- or simply go for the beauty of Shinsen-en itself.

二条城の南側にある神泉苑は、京都の隠れた名所とも言うべき美しい日本庭園です。苑内には、大池、泉、小川、小山、森林などの自然を取り込んだ大規模な庭園が造られており、ここだけで四季折々の景色、雄大な伝統建築、美しい日本の自然風景のすべてを味わうことができるのです。

もともとは8世紀に桓武天皇（かんむてんのう）が平安京に都を移した際につくられたもので、今では当時の10分の1の大きさになってしまいましたが、京都に現存する庭園としては最古のものです。かつて内裏と隣接した13万㎡の広大な敷地は、17世紀初頭に徳川家康が将軍になり、二条城を建設した際に大部分が削られてしまいました。現在は真言宗の寺院で、境内には善女龍王社や、渡ると願い事がかなうという橋などがあります。また、源義経と静御前が出会った場所だという伝説も残されています。なお、池に浮かぶ、船首に龍の頭をいただいた船では、「京都神泉苑　平八」による京料理を味わうことができます。

新緑の美しい5月2日〜4日には、神泉苑祭、紅葉の色づき始める11月には神泉苑狂言が行われます。祇園祭の発祥地でもある1200年以上の歴史をもつ地へ、ぜひ足を運んでみてください。

【神泉苑】
京都市中京区御池通神泉苑東入ル　☎ 075-821-1466　9:00 〜 20:00
市バス・京都バス神泉苑前下車すぐ。地下鉄二条城前駅下車、徒歩3分
【Shinsen-en】
Oike-dōri, Shinsen-en, Higashi-iru, Nakagyō-ku, Kyoto
☎ 075-821-1466　9:00 〜 20:00
http://www.shinsenen.org/

夏

Amazing
KYOTO
Summer

京都盆地の熱気を感じ始めると、
一年で最も賑やかな祇園祭を迎えます。
そして歳時記は夏へと移り変わります。

As heat rises in the Kyoto basin
citizens dress in their finest
and prepare for the busiest
months of festivities.

祇園祭一色の7月は、京都中が沸き立つ最も大事なとき。
とりわけお茶屋さんや見習い芸妓たちの忙しさは格別です。
Apprentice geisha and teahouse staff are hard at work
every summer during the peak of the Gion Matsuri,
with all of Kyoto joining in on the festive spirit.

紫陽花まつり 藤森神社

Ajisai Matsuri | Hydrangea Festival　　Fujinomori Jinja

蹴鞠は平安時代の貴族の間で流行しました。
「アリ」「ヤ」「オオ」と叫んで、言葉でどの
ような動きをするかを伝達します。
Kemari was popular with the noble class in
the Heian Period. Players shout "ari", "ya",
and "o" to declare their intent on the ball
during the game.

この花は建物の近くに生えていて、周りを
カラフルにしてくれます。日本が恋しい。(イタリア)
You see them in small corners of the
building adding colors. Miss u Japan.

One of the beloved staples of a Japanese summer is the sight of colorful hydrangeas (*ajisai*) blooming during the rainy season in June and July. Featuring a wide variety of colors depending on the pH of its soil, large hydrangea bushes make vibrant additions to many gardens, roadsides, and city streets. Many shrines and temples with gardens featuring these flowers hold special events during their peak seasons, where visitors can enjoy the flowers alongside special foods, ceremonies, and performances.

Fujinomori Shrine in southern Kyoto hosts its Hydrangea Festival in mid-June. Each year, the shrine holds special openings of its two hydrangea gardens from the beginning of June for a month's time, with special events such as musical performances, rituals, and sports demonstrations. Though multiple days feature events, the main offerings are performed on the third Sunday. Depending on the year, you can take in a variety of cultural activities such as ritual tea offerings, *taiko* drum performances, a *kemari* ball game, or displays of old court-style instrumentals and dance. With so many different cultural events to enjoy alongside such beautiful gardens, it makes for a wonderful day full of culture and entertainment!

日本の夏の風物詩に、6月～7月の梅雨時期に咲く色とりどりの紫陽花（アジサイ）の風景は欠かせません。土壌のpHレベルによって青や紫などに色が変化する紫陽花は、街路や庭、池などを華やかに彩ります。紫陽花がいちばん美しいのは、雨あがり。多くの神社や寺では、人々が紫陽花の風景を楽しめるよう、見ごろの時期に合わせた特別料理が味わえるイベントや紫陽花にちなんだ行事を行っています。

京都の南に位置する藤森神社の紫陽花苑は1500坪の広さで、3500株の紫陽花が美しい花を咲かせます。6月15日は紫陽花まつり。午前10時から神事が始まり、続いて献花、献茶が執り行われます。毎年6月の初旬から1か月間、ふたつの紫陽花苑を公開して、雅楽、太鼓などさまざまな行事を行います。メインの奉納行事は6月の第3日曜日に行われ、日本の伝統的な「蹴鞠（けまり）」も見ることができます。紫陽花で飾られた枝に挟まれて、鞠が運ばれます。蹴鞠のルールは、右足だけを使って、鞠を落とさないように蹴り続けること。華やかな装束に身を包んだ蹴鞠保存会のメンバーが、軽やかな足技を披露します。この美しい庭と古式ゆかしい行事によって、文化的かつ楽しい素敵な一日が過ごせるでしょう。

【藤森神社】開催日程／紫陽花まつり6月15日　奉納行事6月毎週末
京都市伏見区深草鳥居崎町 609　☎ 075-641-1045
10:00 ごろ～　料金／ 300 円（紫陽花苑）　京阪電鉄墨染駅下車、徒歩 5 分。
市バス藤森神社前下車すぐ。JR藤森駅下車、徒歩 5 分
【Fujinomori Jinja】DATE：Hydrangea Festival・June 15,　Special events・Every weekends in June
609 Fukakusa Toriizaki-chō, Fushimi-ku, Kyoto City　☎ 075-641-1045
Around 10:00　Fee：300 yen (Hydrangea Garden)
http://www.fujinomorijinjya.or.jp/

あじさい寺 三室戸寺

Ajisai-dera | Hydrangea Temple　　Mimuroto-ji

The beautiful temple Mimuroto-ji in Uji is a perfect spot to enjoy the most popular rainy season flower: *ajisai* (hydrangea). Known as the "hydrangea temple", Mimuroto-ji is famous for its extensive garden, which features thousands of hydrangea plants spread out to make for a pleasant stroll among the cedar trees. Over fifty different types of hydrangea are represented, ranging in color from cool blues to shockingly vibrant fuchsia. With a stream and teahouse along the path and the temple behind, this garden is strikingly beautiful and allows for a leisurely trip.

宇治の三室戸寺は有名な紫陽花の名所で、「あじさい寺」として知られています。庭の杉木立の間に何千という紫陽花が華やかに咲き乱れ、よく見る青系の花以外にも50種類以上の紫陽花があり、水色から赤紫までさまざまな色が楽しめます。散策路に流れる小川の風情と寺の背後に広がる豊かな自然が、庭の風景をより一層見事にしています。途中、茶室やベンチもあり、ゆったりとした時間を過ごすことができます。雨の日の紫陽花も格別に美しさを増します。霞のかかった空気の中、花の色はいちだんと鮮やかに浮かび上がります。もしタイミングが良ければ、池に咲く蓮（ハス）の葉に落ちた水滴が水銀のように滑る光景も見られるでしょう。

【三室戸寺】
宇治市莵道滋賀谷 21　☎ 0774-21-2067
8:30 ～ 15:30　料金／ 500 円　京阪宇治線三室戸駅下車、徒歩 15 分
【Mimuroto-ji】
21 Todō Shigatani, Uji City ☎ 0774-21-2067
8:30 ～ 15:30　Fee : 500 yen
http://www.mimurotoji.com/

夏のハイキング 大文字山
Summer Hiking Mt. Daimonji

Part of a larger mountain named Nyoigatake, Daimon-ji is a popular hiking spot. With a height of 465.4 meters, which takes about 45 minutes to climb one-way, even beginners should be able to handle hiking the mountain. The view of Kyoto with the valley spread out beneath is breathtaking, offering a look at how mountains surround and protect the city. The trail lets out in the center of the famous Obon bonfire clearing that gives Daimonji-yama its name, and if you plan your trip well, you can combine your hike with a few local temples and shrines in the foothills.

大文字山は正式には如意ヶ嶽（にょいがたけ）という山の一部分で、標高は465.4mあり、頂上までのハイキングコースはとても人気があります。観光名所の「哲学の道」のすぐ東側にあり、京都中心地から簡単に行くことができます。コースは片道約45分で、ハイキング初心者でも大丈夫。頂上では京都盆地を取り囲む山々が一望でき、かつての都が山々によって守られていた様子がよくわかります。天気の良い日には遠く大阪までも見渡せます。ルートはお盆に行われる「京都五山送り火」の「大（だい）」の形に切り開かれた如意ヶ嶽の中腹部分へと続きます。その中心には名僧・弘法大師ゆかりの小さな神社もあります。事前に下調べをして、東山の麓のお寺や神社をいくつか見て回るのもおすすめです。

【大文字山】
京都市左京区粟田口如意ヶ嶽町
市バス銀閣寺道下車、登山口付近まで徒歩約20分
【Mt. Daimonji】
Awataguchi, Nyoigatake-chō, Sakyō-ku, Kyoto City

京都薪能 平安神宮
Kyoto Takigi Nō │ Firelight Theater　Heian Jingū

能衣装が豪華できらびやか！ 神秘的
な能面にも注目してください。
Take a look at those masks and
magnificent costumes!

👍 7,170 いいね!

ワァー！ 将来、日本に行かなくちゃ！（南アフリカ）
Wow! Need to visit Japan in the future!

Nō (or "noh"), the oldest style of Japanese theater still practiced today, traces its origins back over six hundred years. *Nō* is a highly stylized, ritualistic combination of narrative music and dance, with actors donning rich costumes and masks to portray their roles. Dealing with supernatural and legendary subjects, such as the ghosts of tormented warriors and gods who descend to share a tale with mortals, *nō* performances are usually hours long, composed of four *nō* plays with a *kyōgen* comedy in between. Some *nō* take place at night on a stage lit with torches in a tradition called *takigi nō* ("*nō* by firelight"). Performed on an open-air stage with torches for lighting, Takigi Nō has a dramatic and otherworldly feel.

Kyoto residents and visitors have a chance to take part in such an event every year on June 1st and 2nd at the historic Heian Jingū, a shrine in the Okazaki area of the old capital. If you have the opportunity while in Kyoto and you're interested in the arts, you should definitely take some time to check out *nō* and *kyōgen*!

能は現代も続いている日本最古の舞台芸術です。観阿弥（かんあみ）と息子の世阿弥（ぜあみ）が、室町時代に能の基本をつくったといわれています。この600年以上前に起源をさかのぼる高度に様式化された儀式的な舞台は、音楽と舞で構成され、きらびやかな能衣装と能面をつけた役者が演じます。主に、成仏できない武者の亡霊、市井（しせい）で人間とともに暮らす神、また何かを伝えるために地上に降りてきた神といった、超自然的な存在や伝説を演目のテーマとしています。通常の舞台では「能」が4番と、それぞれの合間に「狂言」という笑劇が演じられ、上演時間は全体で数時間におよぶ、日本が世界に誇る芸術です。

薪能は、日没後に松明（たいまつ）で照らした舞台で演じられます。篝火の炎と野外のステージを利用する薪能はドラマティックで、別世界にいるかのような感覚になります。京都では毎年6月1日と2日に、岡崎の平安神宮でこの薪能が行われ、京都市民、観光客を問わずだれでも見ることができます。まだ伝統芸能を見たことのないあなた、ぜひ京都で能狂言の世界に触れてみてください。

【平安神宮】開催日程／6月1日、2日（予定）
京都市左京区岡崎西天王町97　17:30 ～　料金／有料
市バス岡崎公園　美術館・平安神宮前下車、徒歩5分、地下鉄東山駅下車、徒歩10分
問い合わせ　☎ 075-771-6114（京都能楽会）
【Heian Jingū】DATE：June 1 to 2
97 Okazaki Nishitennō-chō, Sakyō-ku Kyoto City
☎ 075-771-6114（Association）
17:30　Fee：Applies
http://www.kyoto-kanze.jp/takiginoh/takiginoh66.html

田植祭 伏見稲荷大社

Taue-sai | Rice Planting Ritual　　Fushimi Inari Taisha

Held at Fushimi Inari Taisha, the Taue-sai is closely tied to rice cultivation. This Rice Planting Ritual serves as a prayer for a bountiful harvest, featuring men and women in historic farming costumes planting rice to song and dance.

Priests, dancers, musicians, and planters gather in the main hall to perform a ritual offering of food, drink, and performance before proceeding to the sacred rice field, which a priest sanctifies for planting. With dancers performing to a rice planting song, it's fascinating to see the planters in the field working in traditional fashion.

伏見稲荷大社で行われる田植祭は日本の農耕文化と深い関わりがあります。豊作を祈願し、昔の農民姿に扮した男女が歌や音楽に合わせて田植えを行う神事です。伏見稲荷大社の神田に植えられる早苗は、4月12日の水口播種祭（みなくちはしゅさい）で植えられたモミから育てたもの。これを受けて、田植祭が行われるのです。当日は神職、舞手の神楽女、楽師、苗を植える奉耕者が本殿で供物や御田舞を奉納します。その後、神田へと場所を移して、神職のお祓いのあと田植えが始まります。田植え歌に合わせて神楽女が舞い、早乙女たちがひとつひとつ丁寧に手で植えていく様子はとても興味深いものです。

【伏見稲荷大社】開催日程／6月10日
京都市伏見区深草薮之内町68　☎ 075-641-7331　13：00～　料金／無料
JR 稲荷駅下車すぐ。市バス稲荷大社前下車、徒歩7分。京阪伏見稲荷駅下車、徒歩5分
【Fushimi Inari Taisha】DATE：June 10
68 Fukakusa Yabunouchi-chō, Fushimi-ku, Kyoto City
☎ 075-641-7331 13：00　Fee：Free　http://inari.jp

蛍火の茶会　下鴨神社

Hotarubi no Chakai | Tea Ceremony　　Shimogamo Jinja

The Hotarubi no Chakai, or "Tea Ceremony by Firefly Light", has been held at Shimogamo Shrine each June since 1991. On this night hundreds of the blinking insects are released over a stream in the Tadasu no Mori, allowing visitors to enjoy a classic summer night filled with the soft glow of fireflies. In addition to the draw of the atmosphere, the event holds tea ceremonies, traditional dance performances on stage, and a small market selling local specialties. With all it has to offer, the Hotarubi no Chakai makes for a lovely summer night.

蛍火の茶会は、夕暮れに下鴨神社で蛍を眺めながらお茶を味わう行事です。明治時代に御手洗川（みたらしがわ）で催されていたという納涼茶席を復活させたもので、糺の森（ただすのもり）財団が1991年から毎年開催しています。午後5時、門前にて奉告祭（ほうこくさい）が執り行われ、橋殿（はしどの）・細殿（ほそどの）に茶席が設けられます。神服殿では十二単の着付けや箏曲の演奏が行われます。午後8時ごろ、御手洗池の中央に置かれた大きなかごから約600匹の蛍が御手洗川に放たれます。小さな光を放つ蛍が一斉に闇の中を飛び交う様子は幻想的。また、楼門の南側の糺の森で「糺の森納涼市」が催され、和菓子や工芸品など約20の露店が並び賑わいます。

【下鴨神社】開催日程／６月上旬の土曜または日曜（年によって異なる）
京都市左京区下鴨泉川町　☎ 075-781-0010
17：00ごろ〜　料金／無料　市バス下鴨神社前下車、徒歩３分
【Shimogamo Jinja】DATE：Early weekend in June（Varies by the year）
Shimogamo Izumigawa-chō, Sakyō-ku, Kyoto City　☎ 075-781-0010
Around 17：00　Fee：Free
http://kyoto-design.jp/spot/2749?view=event

夏越の祓

平安神宮、上賀茂神社

Nagoshi no Harae |
Summer Purification
Heian Jingū, Kamigamo Jinja

平安神宮の茅の輪。夏越の祓の儀式のひ
とつで、この輪をくぐることで、半年間の罪
や穢れを落とし、心身が清らかになるといわ
れています。
The woven reed *chinowa* at Heian
Shrine awaits visitors who will pass
through it to purify themselves in this
summer ritual.

【平安神宮】開催日程／6月30日
京都市左京区岡崎西天王町97
☎ 075-761-0221
16:00～　料金／無料　市バス京都会館・
美術館前、動物園前下車、徒歩5分
【Heian Jingū】DATE：June 30
97 Okazaki Nishitennō-chō, Sakyō-ku,
Kyoto City ☎ 075-761-0221
Around 16:00　Fee：Free
http://www.heianjingu.or.jp/

茅の輪をくぐろう!

上賀茂神社に設けられた茅の輪。6月の最後の日に「茅の輪くぐり」に参加できます。
The reed ring pictured above is set up at Kamigamo Jinja.

素敵な日本の写真は、ずっと見ていても飽きません。（アメリカ）
I never get tired of looking at pictures of this amazing country.

136

If you've ever visited a Shintō shrine at the end of June, you might have noticed a large ring made of reeds placed on the grounds. These rings, called *chinowa*, make their appearance for the summer rite Nagoshi no Harae, ("Purification Ritual of Summer's Passing"). Traditionally performed on the last day of the 6th month, this purification ritual permits those who pass through the ring to cleanse themselves of misdeeds committed in the first half of the year and to pray for the latter half yet to come.

One explanation of the origin of this ritual comes from an ancient Japanese legend that tells the story of the wandering god Susano'o no Mikoto. One Somin Shōrai, despite being poor, showed the disguised god Susano'o every luxury he could afford when asked for a place to stay the night. In return, Susano'o gave Somin a ring woven from reeds and instructed him to wear it, which then allowed Somin and his descendants to escape plague and illness. Because of this, passing through the large Nagoshi no Harae reed ring is believed to ward off disaster and misfortune.

6月に神社に行くと、茅でつくられた大きな輪が飾られているのに気づくのではないでしょうか？ この輪は「茅の輪（ちのわ）」と呼ばれ、夏越の祓（なごしのはらえ）という夏の儀式のためにつくられます。 儀式は、6月の最後の日に行われ、一年のちょうど半分（初めの6か月）が経過した時期に、半年間の穢れを祓い清めて、残りの6か月の無病息災を祈願するものです。 半年間を振り返りながら輪の前で一礼し、左回り、右回り、左回りと、「8」の字を書くように3回くぐり抜けるのが決まりです。 これを「茅の輪くぐり」と呼んでいます。

この儀式が始まった一説には、旅（放浪）をしていた日本神話の神、スサノオノミコトの伝説が関連しています。 人間に姿をかえたスサノオノミコトが一夜の宿を借りようと、貧しい生活をしていた蘇民将来（そみんしょうらい）にお願いしたところ、蘇民将来はできる限りのもてなしをしました。 そのお礼に、スサノオノミコトは蘇民将来に茅の輪を与えます。 この茅の輪のおかげで蘇民将来と子孫は病気と疫病をまぬがれることができたといわれています。 このことから今日も、茅の輪をくぐることによって、無病息災を祈願することができるのだと信じられています。 神社にある茅の輪はおおむね神社の入口に設けられており、くぐって参拝することができます。

【上賀茂神社】開催日程／6月30日
京都市北区上賀茂本山 339　☎ 075-781-0011
料金／無料　市バス・京都バス上賀茂神社前下車すぐ
【Kaimigamo Jinja】 DATE : June 30
339 Kamigamo Motoyama, Kita-ku, Kyoto City　☎ 075-781-0011　Fee : Free
http://www.kamigamojinja.jp/event/sep.html
http://www.kamigamojinja.jp/english/index.html （English）

火渡り祭 狸谷山不動院
Hiwatari-sai | Fire Walking Festival　　Tanukidanisan Fudō-in

狸谷山不動院の火渡り祭に参加するため、日本各地のさまざまな場所から山伏たちが集まって無病息災を祈願します。
Yamabushi from various areas gather to participate in Tanukidanisan Fudō-in's fire walking festival.

僕も火の上を歩きました。本当にマジカルなところです！（スウェーデン）
I walked too! Truly magical place!

Nestled partway up a mountain in northeastern Kyoto, Tanukidanisan Fudō-in Temple eschews the more traditional Buddhist sect system in favor of the ascetic nature worship of Shugendō. A mountain-based practice that combines various Buddhist, Shinto, and Taoist beliefs, Shungendō can be translated as "the way to spiritual power through discipline". One ritual associated with both Shungendō and Fudō Myō'ō worship is the Hiwatari Matsuri, or "Fire Walking Festival". Held at the end of July at Tanukidanisan Fudō-in, ascetics from around the area gather in full regalia, and wooden prayer sticks called *goma* are assembled into a pyre. With sutra chanting and ritual cleansing using sacred weapons, the mountain monks look quite cool amidst the blazing flames! Once the fire has consumed the *goma*, the still-flaming ashes and remnants are raked flat, and the monks lead the way by walking barefoot across the hot ground before helping the public do the same. This fascinating ritual is not only interesting for its religious components, but also for anyone who would like to participate in a bit of fire walking themselves. Can you handle the heat?

京都の北東の山麓に位置する狸谷山不動院は、交通安全、厄よけ、ガン封じ祈願で知られる修験道の寺です。781年に桓武天皇勅願により平安京の鬼門守護として「吒怒鬼（たぬき）不動明王」が安置されたことが歴史の始まり。1249年には都人の尊崇のため洞窟に安置され、1604年には有名な剣豪、宮本武蔵が修行のためこの地に来たといわれています。武蔵が修行した滝は今でも見ることができます。不動明王の歴史は長いのですが、洞窟を囲むように本殿が建てられたのは1718年のことで、寺としての歴史はそこから始まりました。明治時代の前期に一度洞窟は荒廃しましたが、地域の有志により1944年に現在の形に再興されました。

狸谷山不動院は、仏教、神道、道教の特徴を併せ持つ日本特有の混淆宗教「修験道」の寺であり、山に籠もって厳しい修行を行うことで悟りを得るとされています。修験道と不動明王がつながっている儀式のひとつが火渡りの修行です。この儀式では護摩祈禱のあと、燃え尽きた護摩木（ごまぎ）の上を修験者が渡る荒行が行われます。初めに山伏が熱い灰をならしながら、まだ炎が残っている道を渡ります。山伏が歩いたあと、参詣者もお守りを持って参加します。この儀式は、実際にわれわれも参加できるとても興味深い神事です。

【狸谷山不動院】開催日程／7月28日
京都市左京区一乗寺松原町6　☎ 075-722-0025
19:00 〜　料金／無料
市バス一乗寺下り松町下車、15分
【Tanukidanisan Fudō-in】DATE：July 28
6 Ichijō-ji Matsuhara-chō, Sakyō-ku, Kyoto City
☎ 075-722-0025　Around 19:00　Fee：Free
http://www.tanukidani.com/event/fire_walking/

貴船祭 貴船神社
Kifune Matsuri Kifune Jinja

神輿の行列は森の中を進んで奥宮へ向かいます。奥宮で神輿を頭上に高々と掲げる様子は圧巻です。
Eventually the procession makes its way from the village streets to forest paths towards the inner shrine.

👍 **11,323** いいね!

素敵な祭りとショー！（インドネシア）
Great festival and performance!

Legend says that the goddess Tamayori-hime appeared in Osaka Bay aboard a yellow boat, declaring that a shrine be built and local spirits deified where the boat's journey ended at the river's source. That place is where Kifune Shrine was constructed 1,600 years ago. Kyoto's people looked to Kifune Shrine particularly for matters pertaining to rainfall and harvest. Even today Kifune Shrine remains connected to matters dealing with water, and votive prayer tablets illustrated with horses are offered with prayers.

The first day of June is Kifune Shrine's Kifune Festival. Held at the changing of the seasons, the festival is a lively one with multiple events throughout the day from morning until evening. Rituals are held at the main hall in the morning, and prayers and reports are announced to the gods in the inner sanctuary. The gods' "wardrobe" is also changed to something more befitting of the season. From then, the festivities move into the public eye with a court dance offering before men take to the streets with the portable shrine and head to the inner shrine to put on a show where the serpent Orochi battles the god Susano'o in an *izumo kagura* piece. It may be a bit removed from the city center, but a trip to Kifune Shrine is more than worth the effort!

京都市の北、貴船は、貴船山と鞍馬山のふたつの山に囲まれています。市内より涼しいため、夏の暑さをしのぐには絶好の場所として、ツーリストのみならず、地元の人にも人気です。特に6月1日は「貴船祭」のため、ふだんよりもたくさんの人が訪れます。伝説によると、その昔、玉依姫（タマヨリヒメ）は、大阪湾に黄色い船に乗って現れて、この水源地を求め、淀川を上り、船の終着点として神社を建てて鎮守を祀るよう命令したそうです。この神社は1600年以上前に建立され、現在の貴船神社となりました。祀られている神は水の神。神社ができて以降、京都の人々は雨と収穫に関しての祈りを、この貴船神社に捧げてきたといわれています。飢饉のときには、雨の祈りとして黒馬を奉納し、晴れを望むときには白馬を奉納しました。それが時代とともに板に馬の絵を描いた「板立馬」となり、現在の絵馬へと変化していきました。つまり貴船神社は絵馬の発祥の地なのです。

祭りは本宮での祭典から始まり、雅びやかな舞楽が奉納され、その後、神輿が本宮を出発、町内を練り歩き、奥宮へと向かいます。奥宮では子供たちが神石「船形石」に千度詣りを行います。このあと出雲神楽を貴船神社の神様に奉納します。また日本神話の奇稲田姫（クシナダヒメ）が両親に見送られるシーンから須佐之男命（スサノオノミコト）がヤマタノオロチを退治するまでの物語を再現した出雲神楽の奉納は必見。朝から夜まで、さまざまな神事が行われます。

【貴船神社】開催日程／6月1日
京都市左京区鞍馬貴船町 180　☎ 075-741-2016
11:00 ごろ〜　料金／無料
京都バス貴船、徒歩下車 5 分。叡山電鉄貴船口駅下車、徒歩 30 分
【Kifune Jinja】DATE：June 1
180 Kurama Kibune-chō, Sakyō-ku, Kyoto City
☎ 075-741-2016　Around 11:00　Fee：Free
http://kifunejinja.jp/event.html#6

祇園祭・宵山
四条烏丸周辺
Gion Matsuri・Yoiyama
Shijō Karasuma Area

祇園祭は何回か訪れたことがあります！
すばらしかった！ 最高！（日本）
I have visited Gion Festival
a few times. It is great!
Wonderful!

この祭りはすべての人々が楽しめます。宵山期
間中の山鉾町は「コンコンチキチン」の音色が、
そこかしこで鳴り響いています。
Generations young and old participate in this
extremely popular festival.

Kyoto in July is completely dominated by the Gion Festival, one of the most famous festivals in all of Japan. Begun in 893 and an annual event since 970, the Gion Matsuri is rich with history. From the very first days of the month when local neighborhoods begin organizing to the final day's closing ceremony and purification, visitors to Kyoto would be hard pressed to avoid stumbling into a Gion Festival event.

For three nights before the main parades, Kyoto residents and tourists flock in droves to the Shijō-Karasuma area to celebrate. These nights are called Yoiyama. The streets are pedestrian traffic only during the 15th and 16th, and food stalls line the streets, offering everything from shaved ice to piping hot fried noodles as the sound of Gion Festival music echoes from all directions. During this Yoiyama period, when the floats are lit up and on display for the city to enjoy, everyday people can enter the float headquarters where the relics are displayed like miniature museum exhibitions, purchase lucky charms, and sometimes climb inside the floats to have a look around for themselves. Don't forget your *yukata*!

7月の京都といえば、日本三大祭りのひとつ、「祇園祭」。869年（貞観11年）、京都に疫病や災害が蔓延し、怨霊や疫神の祟りだと恐れた人々が疫病退散の神事として行った「祇園御霊会」から始まりました。970年から京都の年中行事となり、神事にまつわる多くの伝統が今に受け継がれています。

祇園祭は八坂神社の祭礼です。7月初めの吉符入り（きっぷいり）に始まり、各山鉾町で町内関係者によって祭りに関する打ち合わせや、巡行の順番を決めるくじ取式などが行われます。鉾建て（ほこたて）、山建てや曳き初めなど、月末の夏越祭まで京都中が祭り一色となります。

祇園祭の中でもメインイベントといわれる宵山（よいやま）は、「山鉾巡行」前の3日間に行われ、四条烏丸周辺に多数の山鉾が建ち並ぶ様子を楽しみに大勢の人々が訪れます。山鉾巡行の2日前の夜は「宵々山」、前夜は「宵山」と呼ばれています。山鉾町周辺は18時から23時ころまで歩行者天国となります。提灯に灯がともる夜の風情もきれいです。それぞれの提灯に文字やシンボルが書かれており、どの山鉾なのかがわかるようになっています。山鉾町の会所や蔵では、祇園祭にちなんだ屏風などが公開されています。粽（ちまき）を買うと、鉾の2階を見学できるところもあります。祇園囃子の演奏は吉符入りが終わってから練習して、宵山の夜まで披露されます。あちらこちらから流れる生演奏の祇園囃子を聞きながら沿道の屋台で、かき氷や焼きそばなどが買えるのも祭りの楽しみのひとつです。

【祇園祭・前祭宵山】開催日程／7月14日〜16日
四条通り、室町通り、各山鉾町　問い合わせ／☎ 075-752-7070（京都市観光協会）
【Gion Festival Yoiyama】DATE：July 14 to 16
Shijō Kawaramachi, Muromachi-dōri, Each Yamahoko-chō area
☎ 075-752-7070（Association）
http://www.kyokanko.or.jp/gion/

祇園祭・山鉾巡行 四条河原町、新町通り
Gion Matsuri · Yamahoko Junkō
Shijō Kawaramachi, Shinmachi-dōri.

👍 29,649 いいね!

2008 年に祇園祭に参加して、
本当にラッキーでした。
最高に素晴らしい経験でした。(イギリス)
I feel so privileged to have attended the Gion Matsuri festival in Kyoto back in 2008!! It was a truly wonderful experience.

毎年、くじ取り式が行われ、列の並びが決まりますが、長刀鉾は毎年行列の先頭を進みます。
The Naginata-hoko is always at the front of the line, and the other floats hope for a prime spot. Lots are drawn each year to determine the order the floats will take in the parade.

The parade of floats called the Yamahoko Junkō is considered to be the main event of the Gion Matsuri. In the recent past there had been only one parade, but in 2014 it was decided to return to the more traditional practice of having two separate parades- one on the 17th called the Saki Matsuri and one on the 24th called the Ato Matsuri. Twenty-three of the thirty-three total floats participate in the first parade, including ten classified as *hoko* and thirteen as *yama* type floats. Beginning with the Naginata-hoko float at the head of the procession, the sacred child cuts a *shimenawa* rope to signal the beginning of the parade. The floats then make their way down the streets of downtown Kyoto making three large turns called *tsujimawashi*, which are spectacles unto themselves, considering the float wheels do not turn and the giant floats must be physically pulled. Combining the sight of the colorful, art-draped floats and traditional costumes with the sounds of festival music and creaking wooden wheels makes for a parade akin to a moving museum!

祇園祭のメインイベントのひとつといえる「山鉾巡行」は、以前は前祭（さきまつり）のときに1度のみでしたが、2014年から後祭（あとまつり）が復活し、7月17日と24日の2回、行われるようになりました。

前祭では33基の山鉾のうち、23基が巡行します。そのうちの10基は「鉾」、13基は「山」と呼ばれています。鉾先に大長刀をつけているのが「長刀鉾」（なぎなたぼこ）です。今でも稚児の習わしを続けているのはこの鉾だけ。山鉾の順番は、7月2日のくじ取式で決められますが、毎年必ず先頭に立って巡行するのは長刀鉾です。

行列は9時に出発し、稚児の注連縄切りを経て、四条通りから河原町通り、御池通り、新町通りへと巡行していきます。巡行の見どころはやはり通りを曲がる際に行われる「辻廻し」です。水に湿らせた竹を敷いて、呼吸を合わせて、重さ約12トンもの山鉾の進路を変更する様子は圧巻です。都人の優雅な祭りの風情を感じられる祇園祭。祇園囃子の生演奏を奏でながら市中を巡行し、色鮮やかな芸術作品で飾られている山鉾は、「動く美術館」と呼ばれるほど素晴らしい光景です。

巡行のあとは、神幸祭が行われ、神輿が市中を練り歩きます。昼間の山鉾巡行とはまた違って、男たちの活気にあふれる雄壮な姿を見られるのも、祇園祭の見どころと言えます。

【祇園祭・山鉾巡行】開催日程
前祭 7月17日 9：00〜 四条烏丸出発〜四条河原町〜河原町御池〜 11：30ごろ新町御池
後祭 7月24日 9：30〜 烏丸御池出発〜河原町御池〜四条河原町〜 11：20ごろ四条烏丸
問い合わせ／☎ 075-752-7070（京都市観光協会）
【Gion Festival: Yamahoko Float Parade】DATE
Saki Matsuri：July 17, 9:00 〜 11:30
　　　　Shijō Karasuma 〜 Shinmachi Oike
Ato Matsuri：July 24, 9:30 〜 11:20
　　　　Karasuma Oike 〜 Shijō
☎ 075-752-7070（Association）
http://www.kyokanko.or.jp/gion/

祇園祭・花傘巡行 　八坂神社〜四条河原町
Gion Matsuri · Hanagasa Junkō 　Yasaka Jinja ~ Shijō Kawaramachi

On July 24th, the same day as the second Yamahoko Junkō, the Hanagasa Junkō parade sets off from Yasaka Shrine and proceeds around the downtown area accompanied by mounted pages, beauties in kimono, armored figures, and portable shrines before returning to the shrine in the afternoon for a variety of gorgeous performances before the gods and assembled visitors. Though the most famous dances are performed by the *geiko* and *maiko* of the local geisha districts, there are also appearances by *taiko* drum groups, acrobatic *nenbutsu* dancers, and charming children's folk dances.

7月24日朝、山鉾巡行の後祭（あとまつり）が行われるのとほぼ同じ時間帯に八坂神社から花傘巡行が出発します。馬長・児武者、芸妓、舞妓、子どもの神輿などが巡行し、河原町周辺を練り歩きます。その後、八坂神社に戻って美しい舞を奉納します。祇園甲部の芸妓舞妓による雀踊や、地元の子どもたちによる鷺踊などが奉納されます。その日の夕方、還幸祭（右ページ参照）が行われ、山鉾巡行の時期に御旅所（おたびしょ　＊祭りの間、神輿が留まる場所）に着輿した御神輿はそれぞれの地域を賑やかに巡り八坂神社へ戻ります。1か月におよぶ祇園祭のクライマックスを見届けてください。

【八坂神社】開催日程／7月24日
京都市東山区祇園町北側625　☎075-561-6155
10:00 〜 花傘巡行　17:00 ごろ〜 還幸祭、神輿渡御　料金／無料
【Yasaka Jinja】 DATE：July 24
625 Gion-machi Kitagawa, Higashiyama-ku, Kyoto City　☎075-561-6155
10:00 Hanagasa Junkō　Around 17:00 Kankōsai, Mikoshi-togyō　Fee：Free
http://www.gionmatsuri.jp/

祇園祭・還幸祭
Gion Matsuri · Kankō-sai

四条河原町～八坂神社

Shijō Kawaramachi ~ Yasaka Jinja

After the Hanagasa Parade on July 24th, the Kankō-sai celebrates the return of the gods from their temporary resting place (*otabisho*) near Shijō Teramachi back to the Yasaka Shrine. Just as in a procession earlier in the month where they are brought out to the *otabisho*, three groups carry the *omikoshi* around Kyoto downtown, all following different routes before arriving at Yasaka Shrine. Some of the groups go through very narrow streets like the Nishiki Ichiba market, and though carrying those heavy *omikoshi* isn't an easy feat, the local men bring out their best to represent their groups.

7月24日、色鮮やかな祇園祭の花傘巡行（左ページ）のあと、夕方から還幸祭が行われます。八坂神社に祀られる神様が御旅所（おたびしょ）から八坂神社へ戻る神事です。先に行われた神幸祭（7月17日、神輿が八坂神社を出て御旅所へ巡行する）と同じく、神輿を担いだ3つの神興会がそれぞれ市内の別のルートを巡行し、最終地点の八坂神社を目指します。錦市場のような細い商店街を抜けることもあり、沿道の人々は男たちが担ぐ神輿の迫力を間近で楽しみます。重い神輿を担ぐのは容易ではありませんが、地元の男性にとっては名誉な仕事でもあります。

【八坂神社】開催日程／7月24日
左ページ参照。
【Yasaka Jinja】 DATE：July 24
See pg.148

京の七夕 堀川（二条城周辺）、鴨川周辺
Kyō no Tanabata | Star Festival　Horikawa Area, Kamogawa Area

二条から鴨川まで、市中は美しい光に包まれます。浴衣を着る絶好の機会です。（写真は2014年のもの）
From Nijo to the Kamogawa, there are many illuminations lighting up the city and it's the perfect opportunity to walk around in your *yukata*.

👍 5,107 いいね!

素晴らしい写真ですね！ライトが効果的で最高！（オーストラリア）
Wonderful photos!! The lighting effects are magnificent… :)

The story of Tanabata tells the tale of two lovers, Hikoboshi the cowherd and Orihime the weaver, who become so immersed in their love that they stop attending to their heavenly duties. Orihime's father, the Sky God, becomes angry and separates the two by putting the Milky Way "river" between them, allowing them to meet only once a year.

It is said that the period when these lovers meet is prime time to have wishes granted. While people used to pray on Tanabata to improve a certain skill, today people tend to wish for whatever they desire. Because it was held on the seventh day of the seventh month in the lunar calendar, some people celebrate Tanabata on July 7th, and some on August 7th, In Kyoto, the couple's love is celebrated in August with the Kyō no Tanabata!

During the Kyō no Tanabata, Kyoto is lit up at two different event areas. Cleverly woven bamboo spheres illuminated from within sit glowing in the grass by the Kamogawa River, and along the Horikawa River a "bamboo and lights" walkway makes it seem as if you're passing beneath a sparkling path of stars. Public performances of various music, as well as traditional geisha dances and art demonstrations, give visitors plenty to enjoy while strolling through the gorgeously colored night.

七夕にまつわる、「織女と牛飼い」の物語はご存じですよね？ この七夕は、もともと中国のラブストーリーがもとになっています。「牛飼い」とは、わし座のアルタイルという恒星のことで、彦星とも呼ばれています。「織女」はこと座のベガで、織姫と呼ばれています。出会って恋に落ちたふたりは恋愛に夢中になり、仕事が手につかなくなってしまいました。それを見かねた織姫の父親は、空に巨大な天の川を流してふたりを引き離します。これ以降、織姫と彦星は、鳥たちが橋を架けてくれる7月7日、一年に1度しか会えなくなりました。彼らにはスカイプも携帯電話もありません。なかなかたいへんな遠距離恋愛をしていたと思うと、ふたりの逢瀬がよりロマンティックに思えてきます。

ふたりが出会う七夕の日、私たちの願い事も一緒に叶うと信じられています。昔の人々は仕事などの技術の上達を願いましたが、今は特にこだわりはないようです。家族の幸せや、宝くじに当たるようになど、何でも好きなことを祈ります。正式には陰暦の7月7日ですが、陰暦と関係なく7月7日に七夕を祝う人が多くなりました。

京都では8月に「京の七夕」として市全体でイベントを開催します。鴨川の河川敷、堀川遊歩道など、市内各所でライトアップも行われます。

【京の七夕】開催日程／8月前半
京都市中京区二条通堀川付近及び三条川端
19:00〜21:30ごろ 地下鉄二条城前駅下車すぐ（堀川会場）。地下鉄三条京阪駅下車すぐ（鴨川会場）
問い合わせ／☎075-222-0389（京の七夕実行委員会事務局）
【Kyō no Tanabata】 DATE：10 days in early August
Around Nijō-dōri, Horikawa, Nakagyō-ku, Kyoto City Around Sanjō Kawabata, Sakyō-ku,
Kyoto City Around 19:00〜21:30 ☎075-222-0389（Committee）
http://www.kyoto-tanabata.jp/

竹伐り会式 　鞍馬寺
Takekiri-eshiki | Bamboo Cutting Ritual 　Kurama-dera

ホラ貝の合図で、竹を切る大惣仲間（おおぞうなかま）と僧侶の列がそれぞれ本殿に向かい、儀式が始まります。
When the ritual begins, two groups, the bamboo cutters and the monks' retinue, make their way to the main hall after conch shell trumpets signal to start.

 7,983 いいね！

こんな習慣があるなんて知らなかったです。素晴らしい！（ポルトガル）
Didn't know such a ritual existed but it's so awesome!

Every year on June 20th, the monks and locals of Kurama Temple in northern Kyoto gather for their annual bamboo cutting ritual, the Takekiri-eshiki (or Takekiri-e). Held as homage to a legend about Kurama-dera's founder and his battle with demons and serpents on the mountain, as well as a form of divination regarding the crop futures in surrounding areas, the Takekiri-e is a fast-paced and exciting ritual to behold.

After the procession of participants arrives, the bamboo is cut to equal size and a memorial service is held inside the main hall to express gratitude to nature, grain, and water. A performance of *bugaku*, old court-style dance, serves both as offering to the deities and entertainment for those waiting outside who cannot see into the service. The main event, however, occurs when two groups of local men dressed as warrior monks, representing the Omi and Tanba regions, compete to see which team can cut the thick bamboo poles into six pieces first. When these bamboo "serpents" are summarily defeated, which region will have better crops is foreseen. Quite action-packed, this ritual stands out from more sedate ceremonies. And, for those who are interested in nature as well, mountainous Kurama Temple's Takekiri-e may provide just the thing.

京都の北に位置する鞍馬寺は、豊かな自然に囲まれた鞍馬山にあります。770年に中国の僧侶・鑑禎（がんちょう ＊鑑真の弟子）が鞍馬山の草庵に毘沙門天像を祀ったのが鞍馬寺の起源です。もともとは天台宗の寺でしたが、その後鞍馬山の信仰の原点に立ち返り、独自の宗派、鞍馬弘教を設立しました。祀られているのは毘沙門天王、千手観世音菩薩、護法魔王尊の三身一体の「尊天」で、宇宙の大きな力です。また、鞍馬山には自然界を守る山の精霊である天狗が住んでいるといわれています。立地からも鞍馬寺は自然界と深い関係があり、年中行事は自然に関するものが多いのです。

鞍馬寺では、6月20日に竹伐り会式（たけきりえしき）が行われます。平安時代に峯延上人（ぶえんしょうにん）が大蛇を退治し、朝廷から遣わされた人夫が龍ヶ嶽に捨てたという故事にちなむ行事です。まずは本殿で自然、穀物、水に感謝するための供養が行われます。次に僧兵の姿をした鞍馬法師が近江・丹波の両座に分かれ、大蛇に見立てた青竹を誰がいちばん早く6個に切るかを競い合います。長さ4m、太さ15㎝近くもある青竹を力と刃を巧みに使って切る様子はテンポが早く、躍動感たっぷり。いちばん早く切り終わって寺務所に着いた座が勝ちとなります。競技中に飛び散る竹のかけらは厄除けのお守りになるとされています。

【鞍馬寺】開催日程／6月20日
京都市左京区鞍馬本町1074　☎075-741-2003　14:00～
料金／300円　叡山電車鞍馬駅下車、徒歩30分
【Kurama- dera】DATE：June 20
1074 Kurama Honmachi, Sakyō-ku, Kyoto City　☎075-741-2003
Around 14:00　Fee：300 yen
http:// www.pref.kyoto.jp/gyoji/k10.html

亀岡平和祭保津川花火大会

亀岡市大堰川緑地東公園

Hozugawa Hanabi Taikai | Fireworks

Kameoka

亀岡平和祭保津川花火大会では、夜空に大輪の花
火が上がり、河川沿いには色とりどりの夜店が立
ち並びます。日本の夏の夜の美しい光景です。
The colorful roofs of food stalls glow beneath
the burst of fireworks at the Kameoka Heiwa-sai
Hozugawa Firework Festival.

ワァー、すごく綺麗！
これだからこそ日本に行きたいです。
WOW, So beautiful!
This is why I want to visit Japan.

Whether it's sparklers held in the hands of local children or large communal festivals hosted by city governments, summer is the time for fireworks in Japan, when hundreds of firework extravaganzas are held all over the country. For those looking to see fireworks, one of the three most well-known options in Kyoto is the Kameoka Heiwa-sai Hozugawa Hanabi Taikai. Even though Kameoka is a bit far from the city center, approximately 75,000 people attend each year.

People often dress up in *yukata* to enjoy the fireworks and the festive atmosphere, and hundreds of food and drink stalls make sure no one goes hungry while waiting for night to fall and the fireworks to begin. Set alongside the Hozugawa River, the firework festival is free to enter—although reserved seating is available for 1,000 yen. No matter where you sit, however, the sight of 5,000 colorful fireworks bursting in the night sky over a sea of glowing *yattai* stalls is one you won't soon forget!

日本の夏と言えば花火。子供たちが手に持って遊ぶ小さなものから、地域全体で行う大規模な花火大会まで、夏には何百という花火大会が日本中で開催されます。京都市に隣接する亀岡市の花火大会は、60回を超える歴史があり、毎年約7万人以上の見物客が訪れるという大規模な花火大会です。

会場となる大堰川緑地東公園には、浴衣を着た大勢のグループやカップルが花火と夏祭りの雰囲気を楽しんでいます。たくさんの夜店が周囲を明るく照らし、花火大会を盛り上げます。保津川花火大会に入場料は必要ありませんが、よい席を確保したければ有料で特別席を予約することができます。座る席はどうあれ、色とりどりの打ち上げ花火が轟音と共に夜空に大輪の花を咲かせる光景は、あなたの心に深く刻まれるでしょう。

亀岡を満喫したいなら、朝から訪れて、舟に乗って保津川下りをするのもいいでしょう。また川辺でバーベキューをしたり、馬車に乗って散策もできます。古い温泉地でもあるので、周辺の旅館に泊まれば帰りの時間を気にせず、のんびり花火を楽しむことができます。

【亀岡平和祭保津川花火大会】開催日程／8月7日（開催の有無はその年ごとに決定）
京都府亀岡市保津町六条口（大堰川緑地東公園）
料金／無料　JR亀岡駅北口下車、徒歩15分
【Kameoka Heiwa-sai Hozugawa Hanabi Taikai】
DATE：August 7 (Tentative - To be determined every year)
Hozu-chō Rokujyōguchi, Kameoka City (Ōigawa Ryokuchi Higashi Park)　Fee：Free
http://www.kameokacci.or.jp/

花脊松上げ 花脊
Hanase Matsu-age | Fire Festival Hanase

間近で見ると迫力の花脊の松上げ。辺り一面、火の海のように夜空に舞い上がる光景が見事です。
The field filled with torches at the Hanase Matsu-age looks like an ocean of light in the darkness.

いつまでも京都が大好きです！（インドネシア）
I LOVE KYOTO FOREVER.

A prime example of an ancient rural tradition still practiced in Kyoto, the Matsu-age ritual in Hanase Village is one of three fire rituals faithfully preserved in the nearby mountain communities. Held on a hot summer night as part of Obon rituals that honor the spirits of the dead, the Matsu-age in Hanase consists of local men hurling small, flaming bundles of wood at a giant wooden torch 20 meters tall. Set in a field littered with torches and bonfires burning bright in the pitch black night, the men throw their flying kindling high until someone manages to light the torch on fire.

The crowd's reaction is one of the most exciting parts, with voices rising and falling along with the flames until the fire grows large enough to send the torch crashing to the ground. Though it does serve some functions for the Obon season, the Matsu-age is also said to ward off evil spirits that cause fire, as well as promote the growth of crops.

For those looking to get into the more rustic surroundings of the mountains, Hanase, Kumogahata, and Hirogawara all hold variations of the Matsu-age just waiting to be discovered. Depending on how long it takes to light the flames, the event can end quite late, so be careful when it comes to transportation.

8月の炎天下のある日、街の喧騒を離れて京都から1時間半ほどの道のりを経てたどり着く山間の村が花脊(はなせ)です。わざわざ訪れる人々の目的は、大昔から行われている有名な火祭り「松上げ」です。これは洛北の山村に伝わる神事です。花脊周辺の家には、高張り提灯が掲げられ、河原には多数の松明(たいまつ)が準備されます。

祭りではおよそ2,000人の見物客が見守るなか、地元の男たちが高さ20mの巨大な松明(たいまつ)に向かって、火のついた小さい松明を放り上げます。彼らが小さな松明をくるくると投げるたびに観衆から大歓声が上がります。やがて巨大な松明に移った炎は全体を包んで大きく燃え上がり、松明が地面に崩れ落ちるときに祭りはクライマックスを迎えます。大笠が燃え尽きるころ、祭りの一団は伊勢音頭を歌いながら春日神社を目指して歩いて行きます。「松上げ」は先祖供養のために行われる「お盆」行事の一環で、家を火災から守り、秋の豊作が約束されると信じられています。

繁華街とはまた違った京都の田舎の雰囲気に浸りたいなら、花脊、雲ヶ畑、広河原の3つの村で行われる松上げがおすすめです。夜遅くなることもあるので、帰りのバスの確認や、レンタカーなどの移動手段を確保しておきましょう。

【花脊】開催日程／8月15日
京都市左京区花脊八桝町
21:00 ごろ〜　料金／無料　京都バス花脊交流の森前下車すぐ
問い合わせ／☎ 075-746-0127 (花脊保存会)
【Hanase】DATE：August 15
Hanase Yamasu-chō, Sakyō-ku, Kyoto City
Around 21:00　Fee：Free　☎ 075-746-0127 (Association)
http://www.pref.kyoto.jp/gyoji/k11.html

京都五山送り火 　京都市内
Gozan no Okuribi | Obon Bonfires 　　Various Mountains

京都の山々を照らす送り火は、精霊があの世へと戻る道しるべとなります。
The bright bonfires illuminate the mountains of Kyoto and supposedly serve to light the way back to the spirit world for the ancestors who visited for Obon.

興味深い情報です！（モンゴル）
Interesting information!

As part of perhaps the most famous Obon festival in the country, the Gozan Okuribi bonfires are lit on five mountainsides around Kyoto. It is believed that the dead who have come back to visit their living relatives for the Obon period will depart once again for the spiritual world on August 16th, and this is Kyoto's custom for giving them a good send off!

The five *okuribi* (send-off fires) consist of the kanji character for "big" on two mountains, two kanji that form "wondrous dharma" on two others, and two bonfires made into shapes- visible as a *torii* gate and a boat. The most well-known "big" character, Daimonji, is made up of "strokes" of bonfire 160, 120, and 80 meters long! When all the fires are lit, people gather in the streets, along the river, and in tall buildings to catch a glimpse of as many fires possible.

Because of this ritual's long and mysterious history, there are many interesting superstitions about the Gozan Okuribi. It's said that by drinking *sake* or water with the burning bonfires reflected on its surface you will be protected from ailments such as paralysis. Many people also go to temples to write *gomagi*, prayers on cedar strips, to be burned with the bonfires and hopefully reach heaven with the rising smoke.

日本にはさまざまな方法でお盆にお精霊さんを見送る儀式や伝統があります。中でも最も有名なのが「京都五山送り火」です。お盆の時期、家族に会いに戻ったお精霊さんが、あの世に再び帰るとされる8月16日、京都盆地の山々に点火されます。

5つの送り火は、東山如意ヶ嶽（通称大文字山）、松ヶ崎西山・東山、西賀茂船山、大北山、嵯峨鳥居本曼荼羅山に点火。それぞれ漢字で構成されており、ふたつの「大」がそれぞれの山に、「妙法」の文字がふたつの山にまたがって登場し、残りは「鳥居」と「船」の形が表現されています。市内どこからでも見えるように、送り火はとても大きく描かれています。一番よく知られている「大」の字は、160m、120m、そして80m もの線（画）でつくられています。各送り火の文字は、20時ころからひとつずつ点火され、一度点火されると約30分間に渡って燃え続けます。そして20時50分くらいにはすべての送り火が終了します。京都中の人々は少しでも多くの送り火を見るために道に出たり、鴨川のそばに行ったり、高いビルやホテルに集まります。

この儀式は歴史も長く、たくさんの面白い言い伝えが残されています。たとえば、盃の水に送り火の大の字を映して飲むと願い事が叶い、または無病息災に暮らせるといわれています。お盆の時期に京都に行ったら、夜の送り火を見ていにしえの人々に思いを馳せてみてください。

【京都五山送り火】開催日程／8月16日
京都市内各区　20:00 ～ 20:30 ごろ
【Kyoto Gozan no Okuribi】 DATE : August 16
Kyoto City　20:00 ～ 20:30
http://www.kyokanko.or.jp/okuribi/

燈明会　高台寺

Tōmyō-e | Obon Illumination　Kōdai-ji

Located in Higashiyama, Kōdai-ji, established in 1606, is a historic temple associated with Toyotomi Hideyoshi and his wife, Nene. Featuring lush maple trees that change colors with the seasons, the gardens also contain a pond, teahouses, a bridge, and a bamboo grove. For those who want to visit after dark in summer, an illumination is held from August 1st to 18th from sunset to 9:30 pm. The path to the temple is lit by numerous rows of paper lanterns, and the soft glow of lights throughout the garden makes for a very different visit than one you could enjoy in the light of day.

美しい日本庭園と華麗な建築物で人気の高台寺は、1606年創建、豊臣秀吉と妻ねねゆかりの寺として知られています。8月上旬、高台寺では夜間のライトアップが行われ、伝統建築や庭園がまるで絵画のように夏の夜に浮かび上がる光景が見られます。ライトに照らされたモミジの葉影を映した石畳の道は、山麓にある境内の堂宇（どうう ＊格式を備えた寺の建物）や茶室の間を縫うように続き、夜の竹林へと吸い込まれそうな雰囲気。寺社の多くは17時に閉門するので、高台寺のライトアップは一日の観光をさらに長く楽しめる機会でもあります。夜のお寺は昼間とはまた違った美しさと趣です。

【高台寺】開催日程／8月1日〜18日
京都市東山区下河原町526（下河原町八坂鳥居前下ル）☎075-561-9966
日没〜21:30ごろ　料金／600円　市バス東山安井下車、徒歩5分。
京阪祇園四条駅下車、徒歩13分
【Kodai-ji】DATE：August 1 to 18
526 Shimokawara-chō, Higashiyama-ku, Kyoto City　☎075-561-9966
Around Sunset 〜 21:30　Fee：600 yen　http://www.kodaiji.com/lightup.html

季節で砂の紋様が変わります

夏の庭・白砂壇　法然院
Byakusadan | Garden in Summer　　Hōnen-in

Hōnen-in, named for the famous priest who founded Pure Land Buddhism and constructed in 1680, is a quiet temple hidden away from the main tourist routes. Though not far from a popular street, visitors to Hōnen-in feel as if they've entered a secluded mountain temple in the forest, surrounded by maple trees with dappled sunlight filtering in, slightly shaded from the heat. Known for its scenic main gate and raised sand platforms (*byakusadan*), Hōnen-in makes a serene retreat from the hustle and bustle of summer tourism.

寺の歴史は鎌倉時代初期にまでさかのぼり、法然院という名前は浄土宗の開祖、法然に由来します。本堂は1680年（江戸時代）に法然ゆかりの地に再建されたもので、現在の境内はこのときに整備されました。ふだんはあまり多くの人が訪れることなく、ゆっくりと落ち着いた雰囲気です。春と秋には桜と紅葉の名所として大勢の人が訪れますが、緑の美しい夏も趣があります。山門を入ると両側に砂の舞台があり、表面の模様が季節ごとに変わります。もし日本語を話せるのであれば、「法然院サンガ」という勉強会、コンサートなど地域を巻き込んだ共同プロジェクトに参加しても面白いでしょう。

【法然院】
京都市左京区鹿ヶ谷御所ノ段町 30　☎075-771-2420
6:00 〜 16:00 ごろ　料金／無料（参道まで）　本堂／非公開
市バス錦林車庫前下車、徒歩 10 分
【Hōnen-in】
30 Shishigatani Goshonodan-chō, Sakyō-ku, Kyoto City　☎075-771-2420　6:00〜16:00
Fee：Free（Entrance Fee applies during main hall special opening）　http://www.honen-in.jp/

Summer Gifts in Kyoto!

京の夏のおみやげは？

Uchiwa
団扇

These *uchiwa* from the Kyoto Design House are Gion Festival editions called *kyo-uchiwa*. How cool would it be to dress in yukata and carry these fans around Kyoto during the Gion Festival? *Uchiwa* are often given as gifts; during the Edo Period, they were sold as souvenirs at shrines.

日本の伝統的な団扇（うちわ）は、江戸時代には神社でお土産として売られていました。花柄や家紋の入ったものから、水玉模様、広告、アニメキャラといった現代風のデザインまで、実にさまざまな団扇があります。写真は京都デザインハウスの「京うちわ」（祇園祭エディション）です。軽くてエコで、機能的な昔ながらの道具で、京都の夏を快適に過ごしたいものです。

Katori Senkō
蚊取り線香

Mosquitoes seem to love the hot weather as much as we do, but the black, square-shaped *katori senko* is one way to deal with the not-so-pleasant insects *Katori senko* is traditional incense mosquito repellent that has been used in Japan for many years. The all-natural smoke that rises from the incense should drive away those pesky mosquitos!

黒い箱の中には、「蚊取り線香」が入っています。日本ではおなじみの蚊取り線香ですが、自然素材でつくられた線香から立ち上る煙に夏の風情を感じますね。また、実用品としてだけでなく、インテリアとしても使えます。京都デザインハウスで売っている美しいデザインの線香入れは、家から蚊を追い払う、環境にもやさしい優れものです。

【京都デザインハウス】
京都市中京区福長町 105 俄ビル 1F　☎ 075-221-0200　11:00〜20:00　無休（年末年始、棚卸日を除く）
地下鉄京都市役所前駅下車、徒歩 5 分。地下鉄烏丸御池駅下車、徒歩 8 分
【Kyoto Design House】
Niwaka Building 1F, 105 Fukunaga-chō, Nakagyo-ku, Kyoto City　☎ 075-221-0200
11:00-20:00 Closed：Last weekday of each month and New Year's holiday
http://www.kyoto-dh.com　http://www.tokyo-dh.com/en/（English）

Part 2

京の美味

Delicious Food in Kyoto

舞妓さんを描いたラテアート「舞妓
カプチーノ」は、カフェチャオプレッ
ソ京都みやこみち店の人気メニュー。
近鉄名店街みやこみち内
☎075-671-8807　7:00 ～ 21:30（LO）
This *maiko* café latte is from CAFFÈ
CIAO PRESSO Kyoto Miyakomichi
Store ☎075-671-8807　7:00 ～ 21:30
（LO ＊ last order）

京都を訪れる楽しみは、なんといっても京の美味！
美しい和菓子からお茶目なスイーツまで、遊び心あふれる逸品ぞろい。
また、見目麗しい旬の京料理、京の台所・錦市場、食にちなんだ祭事など、
日本中を虜にしているさまざまな "京都の美味" を紹介します。

One of the pleasures Kyoto offers is surely its delicacies! From gorgeous Japanese style confectioneries to reimagined traditional favorites, Kyoto is filled with numerous delights. Discover aspects of Kyoto's food culture that are taking the nation by storm, including Kyoto's visually aesthetic seasonal dishes, classic cuisine, the Nishiki Market, and rituals associated with food.

和菓子
Wagashi

A veritable feast for the eyes, *wagashi* are traditional Japanese confections that come in many shapes, colors and designs. *Wagashi* are made from various plant based ingredients, with staples including *azuki* (red beans), *kanten* (gelatin made out of seaweed) and *wasambonto* (Japanese sugar). From their seasonal inspiration and delicate design to the thoughtful way they are served, *wagashi* are the perfect example of the beauty and aesthetic of Japanese culture. Here are some examples of the various ways you can enjoy a sweet taste of Japan!

京都にはおいしいものがたくさんあります。甘いものだと季節の花や風景を表現した美しい和菓子がおすすめ。日本人の生活と切り離すことのできない、世界に誇るお菓子です。和菓子の多くは小豆をはじめとした植物性の天然素材からつくられ、比較的ヘルシーなお菓子といえます。京都に来たら、伝統ある和菓子店へ足を運んでみてはいかがでしょう。写真上は、「ツツジ」をかたどった淡い紅色の生菓子。京都に咲くつつじは、深紅から純白までバリエーション豊かです。下の写真は、満開の桜の上に浮かんだ朧月を表わした羊羹。あたたかい空気に包まれた春の夜を思わせます。

【とらや 京都一条店】 ※物販
京都市上京区広橋殿町 415（烏丸通一条角） ☎075-441-3111
9:00 ～ 19:00（平日）、9:00 ～ 18:00（土日・祝）　不定休　地下鉄今出川駅下車、徒歩 7 分
販売は年によって異なります。販売期間は店舗へお問い合わせください。
【Toraya Kyoto Ichijō Store】
415 Hirohashidono-chō, Kamigyō-ku, Kyoto City　☎075-441-3111
9:00 ～ 19:00（Weekends ～ 18:00）Closed：Irregular Holidays
http://www.toraya-group.co.jp/

＊この本で紹介する和菓子は季節ごと・年ごとにデザインなどが替わります。ご了承ください。
＊ The Japanese confections introduced by this book may not be the same every year and every season.
＊ LO means last order.

生菓子
Namagashi

ツツジの生菓子「岩根の錦」。ツツジは江戸時代、庶民の間で大流行し、「ツツジ見」という言葉までうまれました。（とらや 京都一条店）
This confection is in the shape of a beautiful red azalea flower, using "azalea viewing" as its inspiration. (Toraya Kyoto Ichijō Store)

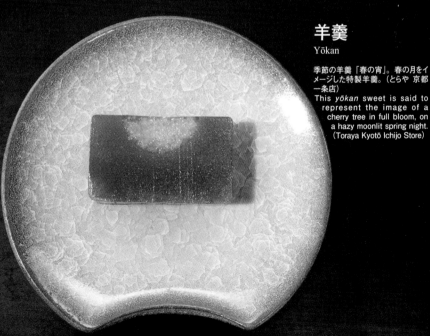

羊羹
Yōkan

季節の羊羹「春の宵」。春の月をイメージした特製羊羹。（とらや 京都一条店）
This *yōkan* sweet is said to represent the image of a cherry tree in full bloom, on a hazy moonlit spring night. (Toraya Kyotō Ichijo Store)

うさぎの饅頭
Rabbit Manjū

なめらかな小豆あんを蒸し饅頭で包み、もち米で質感を出した饅頭。愛らしいうさぎを食べるのは気が引けますが、食べないのはもったいないおいしさ。
(永楽屋本店)

Try a rabbit shaped traditional *namagashi* made with a red bean paste center inside a steamed *manjū* cake topped with shaved sweet rice. (Eiraku-ya Main Store)

若あゆ
Waka-ayu

「若あゆ」は、ワッフルのように焼いた生地をアユの形にして餅を包み、魚の模様を焼き入れた夏限定のお菓子。
(寛永堂三条店)

These *ayugashi* (sweetfish sweets) or *waka-ayu* (young sweetfish) treats are made with a crepe exterior curled around soft rice-cake dough. (Kanei-dō Sanjō Store)

【永楽屋本店】
京都市中京区河原町通四条上ル東側
☎075-221-2318　10:00 〜 20:00　無休
阪急河原町駅下車、徒歩 1 分
【Eiraku-ya Main Store】
Kawaharamachi-dōri, Shijō-agaru,
Nakagyō-ku, Kyoto City ☎075-221-2318
10:00 〜 20:00 7 Days a Week
http://www.eirakuya.co.jp

【寛永堂三条店】
京都市中京区中島町 87（三条通河原町東入ル）
☎075-229-6886　9:00 〜 21:00　無休
京阪三条駅下車、徒歩 5 分
【Kanei-dō Sanjō Store】
87 Nakajima-chō, Nakagyō-ku, Kyoto City
☎075-229-6886　9:00 〜 21:00　7 Days a Week
http://www.kaneido.com

どらやき

Dorayaki

小豆あんをカステラのような食感の生地で包んだ「どらやき」。写真は餡の中に栗が入っています。栗は日本人の大好きな秋の味覚です。（寛永堂三条店）

Here we have a chestnut-filled *dorayaki*, a treat made by mixing red bean paste (*anko*) and *kuri*, then sandwiching it between castella cake. (Kanei-dō Sanjō Store)

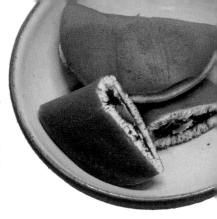

椿餅

Tsubaki Mochi

1000年の歴史を持つ春の生菓子、「椿餅」。椿の葉で挟むことからこの名が付きました。中には小豆餡を包んだ道明寺粉のお餅が入っています。
（永楽屋本店）

Named "*tsubaki*" after the camellia leaves it's served between, this sweet is topped with agar gelatin and has a red bean-paste center. (Eiraku-ya Main Store)

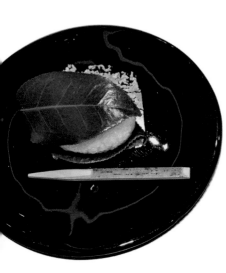

水無月

Minazuki

「水無月」は5月中旬ごろから6月30日限定。米粉に砂糖などを加えて蒸した「ういろう」に小豆をのせた菓子で、抹茶や黒砂糖味もあります。
（永楽屋本店）

This *minazuki* sweet is a steamed cake made of sugar and rice flour called "*uirō*" topped with *azuki* red beans and cut into a triangle.
(Eiraku-ya Main Store)

はろうきてぃ茶寮
Japanese Tea House Hello Kitty Saryō

Japanese-style teahouse Hello Kitty Saryō opened in Kyoto in November 2014, just after Hello Kitty's birthday. Located on Ninenzaka, this adorable restaurant combined with a Hello Kitty goods shop occupies a renovated traditional building that features a lovely tea garden.

The proprietors of Hello Kitty Teahouse seek to combine the fashionable cuteness of Hello Kitty with the seasonal sensibilities and aesthetic of the culture-rich Kyoto. The cute and delicious menu offers everything from small Japanese sweets to full *kaiseki* meals.

西洋だけでなくアジアにも大人気のハローキティ。実はハローキティのレストランが京都にあります。 和風の茶寮「はろうきてぃ茶寮」は2014年11月、ハローキティの誕生月に京都にオープン。高台寺と清水寺を結ぶ、賑やかな二年坂通にあり、素敵な庭がある伝統的な京町家風の建物です。

店のコンセプトはハローキティの可愛さと京都の季節感、日本のお茶文化、そして世界遺産となった「和食」をコラボレートすることです。メニューは、本格的な懐石料理から和菓子まであり、ランチ、ディナー、カフェ使いにも便利。店内は落ち着いた和の空間で、ハローキティのファンならずとも、東山の寺社散策中のひと休みにぴったりです。

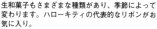

生和菓子もさまざまな種類があり、季節によって
変わります。ハローキティの代表的なリボンがお
気に入り。
There are several choices that change each
season, but we adored this pink and white one
that featured Hello Kitty's trademark ribbon.

生麩パフェのベースはわらび餅、バニラアイス、餡、
カラフルな求肥など。ソフトな生麩でつくったリ
ボンも飾られています。
"Hello Kitty no Oshare Namafu Parfait" is as
stylish as the name claims, with a base of warabi
mochi, vanilla ice cream, and sweet red beans
topped with colorful cubes of *gyūhi* (rice flour
confections), whipped cream, a Hello Kitty
marshmallow and rice cracker, and a ribbon made
from soft and chewy *namafu* (wheat starch).

抹茶ラテにもハローキティのマシュマロと抹茶と
相性のよい干菓子がのっています。
The Hello Kitty Omotenashi Green Tea Latte
features an unbelievably adorable Hello Kitty
marshmallow and comes with some *higashi* dry
sweets to compliment the taste of the *matcha*.

空いていればハローキティと一緒に座れます。
もちろん写真も一緒に撮れます。
You are free to sit across from Hello Kitty
herself if she's free … and of course, she's
always available to appear in your photos!

【はろうきてぃ茶寮】
京都市東山区桝屋町 363-22-2（高台寺南門通下河原町東入ル）
☎ 075-541-1210　10:30 ～ 17:30(LO)　無休　市バス東山安井下車、徒歩 5 分
【Hello Kitty Saryō】
363-22-2 Masuya-chō, Higashiyama-ku, Kyoto City ☎ 075-541-1210　10:30 ～ 17:30(LO)　7 Days a Week
http://www.telacoya.co.jp/kt/

手織り寿し　AWOMB
Hand-Rolled Sushi　AWOMB

With innovative building designs, beautifully landscaped gardens, and stunningly gorgeous food, Japan is known for the creativity and sense of aesthetic it incorporates into everything it creates, and sushi is no exception.

At AWOMB in Kyoto, you can enjoy this beautiful *temaki* sushi set. This work of art presents a plate lined with beautiful ingredients including fresh raw fish and seasonal *kyo-yasai* (Kyoto vegetables), as well as seaweed, a light soup and a glass of Japanese tea.

日本人の創造性と美的センスが生んだ世界に誇る日本食、寿司。寿司は酢飯と生魚を用いて調理され、味だけでなく見た目もよくなければなりません。もちろん自分で握るには修練が必要。でも京都にある AWOMB では具材を自分で巻く「手巻きずし」を簡単に楽しむことができます。

写真の「手織り寿し（ておりずし）」は、新鮮な生魚、季節の京野菜、豚肉や鶏肉などでつくられたおばんざい、海苔、吸い物などがセットになっています。具材を酢飯と一緒に海苔で巻いて食べるのです。人気なので行列覚悟ですが、待つ価値は大いにあります。

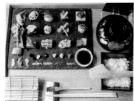

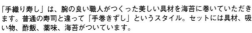

「手織り寿し」は、腕の良い職人がつくった美しい具材を海苔に巻いていただきます。普通の寿司と違って「手巻きずし」というスタイル。セットには具材、吸い物、酢飯、薬味、海苔がついています。
The *temaki* sushi set at AWOMB includes a plate lined with beautiful ingredients that include fresh raw fish and seasonal *kyo-yasai* (Kyoto vegetables), seaweed, a light soup and a glass of Japanese tea.

【AWOMB アウーム】
京都市中京区姥柳町189（蛸薬師通新町通東入ル）
☎ 075-204-5543　12:00 〜 15:00(LO)、18:00 〜 20:00(LO)　無休　地下鉄四条駅下車、徒歩 7 分
【AWOMB】
189 Ubayanagi-chō, Nakagyō-ku, Kyoto City
☎ 075-204-5543　12:00 〜 15:00(LO)、18:00 〜 20:00(LO)　7 Days a Week
http://www.awomb.com

野点 北野天満宮の梅花祭

Nodate | Open-Air Tea Ceremony　　　　Baika-sai, Kitano Tenman-gū

An event that combines Shinto spirituality, seasonal plum blossoms, delicious green tea, and lovely *maiko* and *geiko*, Kitano Tenman-gū's Baikasai (Plum Blossom Festival) is a must-see.

As part of the festival, a *nodate* (outdoor tea ceremony) is performed by *geiko* from the local Kamishichiken District. The ceremony is particularly popular with Kyoto citizens and tourists alike, as it is an opportunity to see a *geiko* up close, and also to be served tea and even exchange a few words.

北野天満宮は学問の神様「天神様」が祀られている京都の北西にある神社です。天神様は九州・大宰府で亡くなった菅原道真公のこと。詩人、学者、官僚として名高く、梅を愛したことでも知られています。境内の梅苑には50種約1500本の赤と白の梅の木があり、毎年2月初旬から3月下旬にかけて公開されます。2月25日の天神様の命日には梅花祭が開かれ、「野点（のだて）」が行われます。上七軒の芸・舞妓が色とりどりの着物と梅のかんざしを身に着け、野外でお茶を点てます。座敷で芸・舞妓と会える機会はなかなかありませんが、この日は抹茶をいただきながら身近に見ることができるチャンスです。

梅花祭には上七軒の芸・舞妓がたくさん参加し、上七軒による野点が行われます。写真は市照さん (p174)、市多佳さん (p175)。
The main attraction of the Baikasai is to take part in the outdoor tea ceremony hosted by the Kamishichiken geisha district. Featured: Ichiteru of the okiya Ichi(pg.174), Ichitaka of the okiya Ichi(pg.175)

【北野天満宮】開催日程／2月25日
京都市上京区馬喰町
☎075-461-0005　10:00 ～ 15:00　料金／梅苑 700 円、抹茶は三連券要 1500 円（3000 枚限定）
市バス北野天満宮下車すぐ
【Kitano Tenman-gū】 DATE：February 25
Bakuro-chō, Kamigyō-ku, Kyoto City
☎075-461-0005　Around 10:00　Entrance Fee：700 yen,　Tea Fee：1,500 yen (Limited to 3,000 people)
http://www.kitanotenmangu.or.jp/

秋のスイーツ
Autumn Sweets

食べてみたいです！（メキシコ）
I need to try it!

Considering the importance Japan assigns to expressing nature through culture, food is always a good indicator of seasons in Kyoto. Chestnut (or *kuri*) is a favorite in autumn, which boasts countless *kuri*-flavored sweets. One such popular treat is the Mont Blanc, a chestnut purée originally from the West. You can also enjoy a mix of flavors, such as sweet potato and chestnut parfait.

街が秋色に染まると、レストランやカフェのメニューも秋らしく様変わり。特に秋のスイーツで人気なのが、栗をピューレにしたクリームを使ったモンブランです。老舗カフェのモンブランは、甘さ控えめで栗の味わいが濃厚。また和菓子店で見つけた秋限定の芋栗パフェは、芋あんの上に栗のアイスと甘露煮、さらにほうじ粒（ハトムギを煎ったもの）とほうじ茶ゼリー、麩やきせんべいとサツマイモのチップス。仕上げには赤いモミジ。見た目も味もパーフェクトです。

1. ヨーロピアンデザートの「モンブラン」は試す価値ありです。（イノダコーヒ 三条支店）
It's worth trying this Japanese twist on a classic European dessert!
2. どこから食べても楽しめる味と食感の「芋栗パフェ」。（永楽屋喫茶室）
Every bite is an interesting combination of flavors and textures.

1【イノダコーヒ 三条支店 】
京都市中京区桝屋町 69 （三条通堺町東入ル）
☎075-223-0171　10:00〜20:00　無休
地下鉄烏丸御池駅下車、徒歩 9 分
【Inoda Coffee Sanjō Store】
69 Masuya-cho, Nakagyō-ku, Kyoto City
☎075-223-0171　10:00〜20:00　7 Days a Week
http://www.inoda-coffee.co.jp/

2【永楽屋喫茶室】
京都市中京区河原町通四条上ル東側 永楽屋本店 2 階
☎075-221-2318　12:00〜18:30(LO)　水曜不定休
阪急河原町駅下車、徒歩 1 分
【Eiraku-ya Main Store】
Eiraku-ya Main Store 2nd floor, Kawaramachi-dōri, Shijō-agaru, Nakagyō-ku, Kyoto City
☎075-221-2318　12:00〜18:30(LO)
Closed：Some Wednesdays
http://www.eirakuya.co.jp

夏のスイーツ
Summer Sweets

京都のお菓子は素晴らしい！ 美味しいし見た目も素敵！
Kyoto sweets is fantastic! Looks good, tastes good.

One way to beat Kyoto summer heat is to indulge in some cool Japanese treats. A popular choice is *kakigōri* (shaved ice), which is a great way to cool off without being weighed down. Green tea is a traditional flavor, but there is a wide variety to satisfy your taste buds. You can also find many Japanese confections with summer festival themes, such as starry sky Tanabata *yōkan*.

日本の夏にかき氷は欠かせません。夏祭りの屋台や、カフェの季節メニューとして、またコンビニでもよく見かけます。日本のかき氷は外国のいわゆるスノーコーンよりももっとふわふわしていて、シロップがかかり、さまざまなトッピングがなされています。京都は有名なお茶の産地なので、小豆のった「抹茶味」や「ほうじ茶味」のかき氷が売られています。また和菓子店では色や素材で涼しさを表現したお菓子を販売します。

1. かき氷の「天然いちごミルク」。(SECOND HOUSE 東洞院店)
The four white balls on the side are *shiratama dango*, a type of dumpling made out of rice flour.
2. 7月7日の伝統行事「七夕」をイメージした羊羹「天の川」。空に揺らめく星を表現。(七條甘春堂)
It might be hard to believe that this is food, but we promise they taste great.

1 【SECOND HOUSE 東洞院店】
京都市中京区御射山町 283 （東洞院通六角下ル）
☎075-241-2323　11:00〜22:30(LO)　無休
地下鉄四条駅下車、徒歩 7 分
【SECOND HOUSE Higashinotōin Store】
283 Misayama-chō, Nakagyō-ku, Kyoto City
☎075-241-2323　11:00〜22:30(LO)　7 Days a Week
http://www.secondhouse.co.jp

2 【七條甘春堂】
京都市東山区西ノ門町 551 （七条通東入ル）
☎075-541-3771　9:00〜18:00　無休
京阪七条駅下車、徒歩 1 分
【Shichijō Kanshundō Main Store】
551 Nishinomon-chō Shichijō-dōri-Higashi-iru, Higashiyama-ku, Kyoto city
☎075-541-3771　9:00〜18:00　7 Days a Week
http://www.7jyo-kansyundo.co.jp/

抹茶フード
Green Tea Sweets

Since Kyoto is known for its green tea, (*matcha*), you can find *matcha* flavored food and beverages on nearly every street corner. Kyoto is where tea from China was first introduced in the 700's, and the quality is still regarded as being the highest in the country. When the bitterness of green tea powder is mixed with something milky or creamy, it becomes the perfect sweet, popular world-wide! You can find traditional Japanese green tea sweets in Kyoto, of course, but why not try something with a bit of a twist, like a stylish parfait, smoothie, or fondue? We definitely recommend you try one or two-or even five-of the popular and interesting *matcha*-flavored delights you can find in the old capital.

「抹茶」はすでに外国人にもおなじみの味ですが、京都にはありとあらゆる抹茶を使った食べ物があります。抹茶アイスクリームから抹茶そば、抹茶のビールまで。特に夏の京都で人気なのが抹茶のパフェ。その味もスタイルも店によってさまざまで、花見小路通りから少し入った場所にある町家カフェ「和バル　OKU」のボリュームたっぷりの抹茶パフェや、行列がたえない「茶寮都路里」の宇治産の高級茶葉を使用したパフェなど、いろいろ食べ比べるのもいいでしょう。グラノーラの専門店「COCOLO KYOTO」では冷たくてクリーミーなスムージーボウルに抹茶フレーバーのグラノーラをトッピングできます。そして八坂神社にほど近い祇園のカフェ「ジュヴァンセル　祇園店」では抹茶チョコレートソースにフルーツなどを付けて食べる抹茶チョコレートフォンデュも！いろいろな抹茶のバリエーションを楽しんで。

美味しそう！上に載っているのはマンゴー？（イタリア）
Yum! Is that mango on the top?!
Looks delicious!

↖ 世界の人が最も " いいね! " した京の味

1	2	3	4

1. 抹茶ムース、ワラビ風味の餅、ラスク、小豆アイスクリーム、サツマイモのチップス、そして抹茶アイスというボリューム。（和バル OKU）The parfait at Oku is made up of green tea mousse, *warabi* rice cakes, rusk cookies and *azuki* ice cream.

2. カステラ、白玉団子、抹茶アイス、そのすべてに京都南部のお茶の産地、宇治で栽培した抹茶が使用されています。（茶寮都路里）Saryō Tsujiri's parfait comes with castella cake, *shiratama dango*, and green tea ice cream- all made with tea from Uji.

3. 抹茶のスムージーボウルの上にマンゴー、ナッツ、ベリー類、抹茶フレーバーのグラノーラをトッピング。（COCOLO KYOTO）The granola sprinkled on this smoothie with the mango, nuts and berries is also *matcha* flavored, as COCOLO KYOTO specializes in granola.

4. 果物、和菓子、抹茶チョコレートソースの祇園フォンデュ。ソースは程よい温度で具と調和します。（ジュヴァンセル 祇園店）This *matcha* fondue set at Jouvencelle Gion-en includes fruit, Japanese sweets and a pot of *matcha* chocolate sauce. The sauce isn't too sweet or too bitter, making it the perfect topping.

---

1 【和バル　OKU】
京都市東山区祇園町南側 570-119
☎ 075-531-4776　11:30 ～ 21:00（L.O.）14:30～
17:00 はカフェタイム　火曜休　阪急河原町下車、
徒歩 4 分
【Wa-baru OKU】
570-119 Gion-machi-minamigawa, Higashiyama-
ku, Kyoto City　☎075-531-4776 11:30～21:00
(L.O) Cafe Time 14:30～17:00　Closed：Tuesday
http://www.oku-style.com

2 【茶寮都路里】
京都市東山区四条通祇園町南側 573-3　祇園辻利
本店 2・3F　☎ 075-561-2257　10:00 ～ 21:00
(L.O.)　土・日・祝 10:00 ～ 20:30(L.O)　無休
京阪祇園四条下車、徒歩 5 分
【Saryō Tsujiri】
573-3 Gion-machi-minamigawa, Higashiyama-ku,
Kyoto City　☎075-561-2257 10:00～21:00(LO)
Weekends/Holidays 10:00～20:30(LO)
http://www.giontsujiri.co.jp/saryo/

3 【COCOLO KYOTO】
京都市中京区木之下町299（姉小路通堺町東入ル）
ENJOY bldg 1F
☎075-229-6619 11:00 ～ 16:00（LO）
火曜休　地下鉄烏丸御池下車、徒歩 5 分
【COCOLO KYOTO】
299 Kinoshita-chō, Nakagyō-ku, Kyoto City
☎075-229-6619 11:00～16:00(LO) Closed：Tuesday
http://www.cocolo-kyoto.jp/

4 【ジュヴァンセル 祇園店】
京都市東山区清井町 482（八坂鳥居前南入ル）
京ばんビル 2F
☎ 075-551-1511 10：00 ～ 17：30(LO) 不定休
京阪祇園四条駅下車、徒歩 8 分
【Jouvencelle Gion Store】
Kyōban Building 2F,482 Kiyoi-chō, Higashiyama-
ku, Kyoto City　☎075-551-1511 10:00～17:30
（LO）Closed：Irregular
http://www.jouvencelle.jp/

駅弁　ジェイアール京都伊勢丹
Ekiben Lunchboxes　JR Kyoto Isetan

Part of the excitement of riding the *shinkansen* is buying a lavish and delicious *bentō* lunch at the station. These *bentō* boxes are called *ekiben*, since "*eki*" means "railway station" and "*ben*" is abbreviated from "*bentō*", meaning "lunch box". It's believed that Japan's first *ekiben* consisted of some *onigiri* (rice balls) sold at Utsunomiya Station in 1885. Now at any large station you will see rows of beautiful *ekiben* lined up in stores. The appeal of *bentō* boxes is that you can buy special *ekiben* made with the local delicacies of the city you're in. Therefore in Kyoto you will find *ekiben* made with special *kyō-yasai* (Kyoto vegetables).

色とりどりの「駅弁」は新幹線に乗るときの楽しみのひとつです。日本初の駅弁は1885年に宇都宮駅で売られていたおにぎりだといわれています。最近では大きな駅に行くと、店によっては150種類以上の弁当を売っていることも。魚介類が有名な札幌では特製カニ弁当、京都では京野菜を使った弁当など、地域の特産品を使った駅弁もあります。ほかにもそば、サンドイッチ、寿司弁当、動物性の食材を一切使わない完全ベジタリアン用の駅弁も。京都駅にあるジェイアール京都伊勢丹で見つけた駅弁をいくつか紹介します。伝統的な押し寿司から現代風のヘルシー弁当まで、いろいろな種類を楽しんでください。

関西地方で定番の押し寿司。写真の「浪花寿司」は、食べやすい一口サイズです（p180 古市庵）。玄米の寿司、サラダ、ベトナム風春巻きなどが入ったヘルシー弁当（写真左／RF1 ガストロノミ）。下の段に鶏そぼろご飯、上の段に豆腐ハンバーグ、かぼちゃなどの煮物などが入った二段重弁当（写真右／まつおか）。
The sushi in this *bentō* are cut up into perfect bite-sized pieces. (pg.180, Kochian)
This healthy lunchbox includes sushi made from brown rice, salad, a Vietnamese style spring roll, and more. (RF1)
These two-layered *ekiben* usually have rice on the bottom and the main dish(es) on top. (Matsuoka)

【ジェイアール京都伊勢丹 B2F「古市庵」「まつおか」「RF1」】
京都市下京区東塩小路町（烏丸通塩小路下ル）
☎ 075-352-1111（大代表）　10:00〜20:00　JR、近鉄、地下鉄京都駅直結
【JR Kyoto Isetan B2F Koichian, Matsuoka, RF1】
Higashi-shiokōji-chō, Shimogyō-ku, Kyoto City　☎ 075-352-1111 (Isetan Main Number)　10:00〜20:00
http://kyoto.wjr-isetan.co.jp
※ここで紹介した駅弁は、年ごと季節ごとに替わります。
※ Ekiben Lunchboxes may not be the same every year and every season.

大根焚き　三寶寺の御会式

Daikondaki | Exorcism Radish　　Oe-shiki, Sanpō-ji

皆さんにふるまわれます！

In December, Sanpō-ji in northwest Kyoto holds it's "Exorcism Radish" ritual (*daikondaki*) which celebrates the death anniversary of the Buddhist sage Nichiren, who founded the sect and promoted the Lotus Sutra as the true way to Enlightenment. Hundreds visit the temple during this event to partake in a bowl of piping hot radish blessed to protect against palsy as well as Sanpō-ji's signature *yuzu* (citron) rice said to warm the body in winter. Throughout the day rituals are also held inside the main hall, including a tea offering and a passionate recitation of sutra.

大根は冬の日本料理に欠かせない食材のひとつ。漬物、薬味などにも幅広く使われます。お寺では冬に大根を煮て参拝者に提供する儀式、「大根焚き（だいこんだき）」を行います。京都の北西にある三寶寺の「厄落としの大根焚き」は、13世紀から続く長い歴史があり、日蓮宗の宗祖、日蓮大聖人の命日に行われます。温かい大根と特製の柚ご飯を食べに何百人もの人が訪れます。大根は厄落としの祈祷として、柚は冷えた体を温めるため食べられるようになりました。本堂では献茶式、厄落としの祈祷、妙法蓮華経の御経読みなどさまざまな儀式が行われます。この寺は1626年に後水尾天皇の命令で創建。茶道宗徧流の流祖で、後に赤穂浪士の討ち入りを助けた山田宗徧（やまだそうへん）がここで奥義を極めたと言われています。

厄落としの祈祷の「食べられるお守り」が釜に入れられます。「寺内」で食べる方は漆器で出され、大根、京豆腐、柚ご飯を楽しめます。
Edible charms to prevent palsy and other forms of paralysis are placed in to the vats. Served in laquerware for those "eating in", you can enjoy healthy boiled radish and Kyōtofu and finish it off with the pleasantly tart citron rice!

日本の大根が恋しくなりました。
I miss Japanese daikon.

【三寶寺】開催日程／12月第1土曜日・日曜日
京都市右京区鳴滝松本町32　☎ 075-462-6540　10：00～15：00　料金／大根焚き700円
市バス福王子下車、徒歩20分。JRバス三宝寺下車、徒歩5分
【Sanpō-ji】DATE：First weekend in December
32 Narutaki Matsumoto-chō, Ukyō-ku, Kyoto City
☎ 075-462-6540　Around 10:00~15:00　Daikondaki　Fee：700 yen
http://www.sanbouji-kyoto.or.jp

冬の定番
Winter Soul Food

> ぼたん鍋、すごく美味しそうで，おなかがすいてきました（メキシコ）。That looks so great, now I'm hungry.

ぼたん鍋
Boar Stew

Dining on *onabe* (pot dishes) is a great way to enjoy winter. This is *botan nabe*, which contains wild boar. You can enjoy this *nabe* at Kurama Onsen, a place in the mountains where you might actually see a boar yourself!

海外にあまり知られていない日本料理のひとつに、イノシシ肉を使った「ぼたん鍋」があります。冬にみんなで囲む鍋は日本人にとって格別ですね。写真は京都郊外にあるくらま温泉で人気のミニぼたん鍋セット（1人前）です。この山ではイノシシが見られるかも。

【くらま温泉】　冬季限定
京都市左京区鞍馬本町520　☎ 075-741-2131
11:00 〜 20:00(LO)　無休　ぼたん鍋（1人前小鍋セット）2600 円〜
叡山電車鞍馬駅より無料送迎バスあり
【Kurama Onsen】 DATE : Winter Only
520 Kurama Honmachi, Sakyō-ku, Kyoto City
☎075-741-2131　11:00〜20:00(LO)
7 Days a Week　http://www.kurama-onsen.co.jp/

年越しそば
New Year's Eve Buckwheat Noodles

This special soba is called "*toshikoshi*" *soba*, which means "end the old year and enter the new year" buckwheat noodles. It is customary to eat these *soba* noodles with family on New Year's Eve.

「一年を締めくくり、新しい年を迎える」という意味を持つ「年越しそば」。そばは長寿と幸運を招くともいわれています。12月31日の夜に家族そろって食べる習慣があります。写真は京都名物の「にしんそば」です。

【総本家にしんそば松葉】
京都市東山区川端町192　☎ 075-561-1451
10:30 〜 21:00(LO)　水曜休　京阪祇園四条駅下車すぐ。阪急四条河原町駅下車、徒歩 5 分
【Sōhonke Nishin Soba Matsuba】
192 Kawabata-chō, Higashiyama-ku, Kyoto City
☎ 075-561-1451　10:30〜21:00(LO)
Closed : Wednesday
http://www.sobamatsuba.co.jp/

ぜんざい
Sweet Red Bean Soup

Nothing says "sweet and delicious" during winter in Japan like a hot bowl of *zenzai*! A variety of red bean soup (*oshiruko*), *zenzai* is made from both whole and ground red beans, giving it a jam-like texture.

冬の 「甘くておいしい」 もののひとつにぜんざいがあります。 おしること似ていますが、 つぶし餡を使うのでジャムのような食感。 お口直しには塩昆布や梅干しを。

甘酒
Sweet Sake

Amazake, or "sweet *sake*," can be alcoholic or not depending on the recipe, and is often seen in Shinto rituals, particularly around New Years when a hot cup is just the thing you want to warm your bones.

祇園・八坂神社の 「をけら詣り」 の目的は、 神前に捧げられた 「をけら灯籠」 の火を縄に移して持ち帰ること。 新年最初のかまどの火として使うのです。 もうひとつの楽しみが甘酒。 初詣でで冷えた体を芯から温めてくれます。

【八坂神社】 開催日程／1月1日
京都市東山区祇園町北側 625　☎ 075-561-6155　大晦日から元旦　境内自由
【Yasaka Jinja】 DATE：January 1
625 Gionmachi Kitagawa, Higashiyama-ku, Kyoto City ☎ 075-561-6155
New Year's Eve/Day　Entrance Fee：Free
http://www.yasaka-jinja.or.jp/

餅つき 京都ゑびす神社

Mochitsuki | Making Mochi   Ebisu Jinja

One of the events held on the first day of Tōka Ebisu is a *mochitsuki*, or *mochi* making event. Surrounded by festival attendees, the priests and priestesses of the shrine bring out the traditional mallet and mortar, as well as a huge amount of piping hot sticky rice just waiting to be pounded! Watching the powerful swings of the mallet and the skillful turning of the rice dough is exciting, since the steam rising off the *mochi* promises a nice warm treat to come. Once the priests have hammered it into shape it's handed off to the priestesses, who shape it into the bite-sized pieces we all enjoy.

各地の神社では新年に餅をつき、参拝者に ふるまいます。中でもお正月の大きなイベン トは、1月8日から12日まで祇園近くのゑびす 神社で催される「十日ゑびす大祭」(p70参 照)です。ゑびす様は漁業と商業の守り神 様。ビジネスマンや商店主らをはじめ、多く の人々が参拝し、幸運と富を呼ぶ「福笹」 を求めて訪れます。餅つきは十日ゑびす大祭 の初日に開催。見物客に囲まれた神職がリ ズミカルに杵を振るい、もうひとりがタイミング よく、蒸した熱々のもち米をひっくり返してい く様子は圧巻です。このときできた餅は11日 に行われる「残り福祭」で「福餅」として 参拝者に振る舞われます。

餅つきは年末年始に各地域で行われる日本の
伝統的な行事です。機会があればぜひ挑戦し
てみてください。
Mochitsuki is a very popular community
event in Japan, especially around New
Year's season. If you have a chance, you
should take a swing at it yourself.

私はお餅が大好きすぎて、愛犬の名前に「モ
チヒメ」と名付けました。（アメリカ）
I love mochi! That is why I named my
dog "Mochi-hime" :)

【ゑびす神社】開催日程／1月8日
京都市東山区小松町 125（大和大路通四条下ル）
☎ 075-525-0005　9:00 ～ 23:00　※餅つきは 14:30 ～
京阪祇園四条駅下車、徒歩 6 分。または市バス河原町松原下車、徒歩 5 分
【Ebisu Jinja】DATE：January 1
125 Komatsu-chō, Higashiyama-ku, Kyoto City
☎ 075-525-0005　9:00 ～ 23:00　Mochitsuki 14:30
http://www.kyoto-ebisu.jp

ぜんぶ試してみたい！おいしそう！
Love to try them all! Yum!

錦市場
Nishiki Ichiba   Nishiki Market

At Nishiki Market you can enjoy delicacies from not only Kyoto, but all around Japan. Situated right in the middle of the old capital, the market street boasts over 120 stores specializing in food and kitchenware.

All of the senses are heightened when entering this vibrant market. With shop assistants calling out *"irasshaimase"* ("welcome"), you can smell tantalizing aromas as you walk past each store. Your taste buds get a good workout with all the amazing food samples, and while touching the displayed food before buying is not recommended, experience with your eyes the beautiful, the interesting, and the downright "what is *that*?" food at the market.

「京の台所」として知られる錦市場は錦小路通沿いに390mにわたって続いています。京都だけでなく、日本中の味が楽しめ、食品以外にも食器や調理道具の店など120軒以上の専門店が建ち並んでいます。1311年ころ、このあたりで数軒の魚屋が商売を始めたのが始まりといわれています。その後、果物、野菜、漬物、茶、菓子、寿司、香辛料…と店舗を増やしてきました。多くのお店は数世代続く家族経営で、長い歴史を感じさせます。活気に満ちた通りに足を踏み入れれば一気にテンションが上がります。おいしそうなもの、珍しいもの、不思議なものが店頭に並び、目を楽しませてくれます。お土産選びはもちろん、食べ歩きも楽しみのひとつ。各店でその場で食べられる総菜やおやつをそろえています。おなかを空かせて市場に入っても、通りを出るころにはおなかも心も満足していることでしょう。

錦市場で買える
面白フード！
（おもしろ）

七味アイスクリーム
Spicy Shichimi Ice Cream

七味は7種の材料でつくられたスパイスです。最初はバニラのような味ですが、次第に口の中で燃えるような辛さに変わります。

A creamy vanilla ice cream hides a strong *shichimi* seven spice punch.

せんべい
Senbei on a Skewer

錦市場では1枚ずつせんべいを買うことができます。食べ歩きしやすいように串がついているものもあります。

At Nishiki you can find large *senbei* sold individually to eat while walking.

串タコ
Octopus on a Skewer

このタコの中には何とうずらの卵が！クリーミーな黄身の食感はタコと絶妙に合います。

This octopus on a stick has a delicious quail egg surprise inside.

ゴマ団子
Sesame Balls

このゴマ団子の中にはピーナツバターに似た風味の黒ゴマ餡が入っています。

Sesame balls with golden sesame on the outside have black sesame paste on the inside.

刺身
Sashimi on a Skewer

串に刺したお刺身まであります。マグロやイカなどの魚介があります。

Try delicious, bite size salmon *sashimi* on a skewer with a dash of lemon juice.

漬物
Pickled Japanese Vegetables

漬物には塩漬け、酢漬け、味噌漬けなどたくさんの種類があります。

You can smell, taste, and buy different kinds of pickled Japanese vegetables at Nishiki.

【錦市場】
京都市中京区錦小路通寺町〜高倉間　地下鉄四条駅下車、徒歩3分
【Nishiki Ichiba】
Nishikikōji-dōri, Teramachi—Takakura, Nakagyō-ku, Kyoto City
http://www.kyoto-nishiki.or.jp/

餅上げ
醍醐寺の五大力尊仁王会
Mochi-age
Godai Rikison Ninnō-e, Daigo-ji

Each February, men and women test out their muscles by lifting large cakes of *mochi* (rice cakes) at the Mochi-age event at Daigo-ji. It sounds easy, but men have to lift 150 kilograms of delicious *mochi*— and women, 90 kilograms. The challenger who manages to hold the *mochi* for the longest time is the winner.

The Mochi-age is part of the Godai Rikison Ninnō-e ceremony. During this period, the priests ask for power from the Five Wisdom Kings in order to pray for peace, health, and happiness, with the Mochi-age being an offering of a feat of strength gifted to the Buddhist deities.

力自慢の方はぜひ、醍醐寺で行われている「餅上げ」に挑戦してみてはいかがでしょう？一見、簡単そうに思われるかもしれませんが、男性は150kg、女性は90kgの餅を持ち上げられるかを競います。いちばん長く持っていられた挑戦者が優勝です。賞品は何かというと… もちろん五大力尊の幸運のお餅です！

年齢も体格もさまざまな男女が挑戦し、餅チャンピオンを目指します。挑戦者は歯を食いしばり、うなりながら巨大な餅と格闘します。楽しんで参加する人もいれば、真剣そのものの人も。餅上げは五大力尊仁王会という醍醐寺最大の年中行事のひとつで、五大明王の力を借りて国家の平和と、国民の健康と幸福を願う力を供物として仏に捧げる儀式なのです。

醍醐寺では、毎年 2 月 23 日に男女が集まって巨大な餅を持ち上げて力試しを行います。「五大力さん」と親しまれている行事です。
While some participants try to lift for fun, others take it quite seriously as a religious ritual.

この女性たちは強いですね！
These girls are really strong.

【醍醐寺】開催日程／2 月 23 日
京都市伏見区醍醐東大路町 22　☎ 075-571-0002　地下鉄醍醐駅下車、徒歩 15 分
【Daigo-ji】DATE：February 23
22 Daigo Higashiōji-chō, Fushimi-ku, Kyoto City　☎ 075-571-0002
https://www.daigoji.or.jp

Character Bentō!

★ キャラ弁に挑戦！ ★

👍 30,835 いいね!

「キャラ弁」とは、「キャラクター弁当」の意味で、人気のアニメキャラクター、動物、花などを具材で表現したお弁当のこと。写真のキャラ弁は、「Kyoto Fan」スタッフがつくったお弁当です。おいしさはもちろん、かわいらしい舞妓さんの形（写真右）になっているのはお見事！

These cute lunch arrangements are called "*kyaraben*". *Kyaraben* (shortened from "character bentō") means "character lunch box" and describes lunch boxes decorated to look like people, characters from popular animation, animals, and plants.

髪は海苔、顔はご飯、着物は卵、ハムなどの具材で表現しています。
The hair is made of seaweed, the face from rice, and the kimono is composed of delicious ingredients like egg, ham, crabmeat, and cheese… yum!

子供のためにこのお弁当をつくってあげたいです。
（スリランカ）
I'll try to make this for my kids. Nice bento!

TOURIST INFORMATION
京都の観光サービス案内は次のとおりです。

【京都総合観光案内所（愛称・京なび）】
豊富な観光資料を取りそろえ、語学力の高い案内経験を
積んだスタッフが常駐し、観光案内、相談、観光情報発
信、観光関連チケット販売、宿泊紹介・斡旋を行ってい
る。英語、中国語、韓国語対応。無料Wi-Fiあり。
住所／京都市下京区　京都駅ビル2階　南北自由通
路沿い
時間／8:30～19:00（年中無休）
☎075-343-0548(おこしやす)
www.kyokanko.or.jp/kyonavi_open.html

【関西ツーリストインフォメーションセンター　京都】
JTB西日本運営の京都タワー内観光案内所。京都、関
西から日本全域まで紹介。お得な交通パス、日帰りツ
アー、入場観覧券、SIMカードなど販売。宿泊予約。無料
Wi-Fi、無料インターネットサービス、ATM、外貨両替機あ
り。英語、中国語、韓国語対応。
ホテルへの手荷物当日配送、一時預かり、宅配も行う。
休憩スペース、礼拝堂あり。日本文化体験・紹介・各種イ
ベント（期間限定）。
住所／京都府京都市下京区東塩小路町721-1 京都タ
ワー3階（烏丸通七条下ル）
☎075-341-0280
FAX075-341-0281
時間／10:00～18:00〈12/30～1/3 は休み〉
www.tic-kansai.jp

【京都市観光協会】
京都の豊かな観光資源を活用した観光事業の企画運
営。国内外への京都の紹介宣伝、観光案内などを行って
いる。
☎075-752-7070
http://www.kyokanko.or.jp/

【京都観光Navi】
京都観光のオフィシャルHP。「Kyoto Official Travel
Guide」とリンク接続し、13か国語で対応。
http://kanko.city.kyoto.lg.jp/

【Kyoto Tourist Information Center　(Kyonabi)】
Languages：English, Chinese and Korean
Wi-Fi：Available for free
Internet PC：Available for a fee
Address：Kyoto Station Bldg. 2F, Shimogyō-ku,
Kyoto City
☎075-343-0548
Hours：Open daily from 8:30 to 19:00

【Kansai Tourist Information Center】
This center is managed and operated by JTB Western
Japan, Corp, Japanese travel agency
Guidance Area：Kyoto, Osaka, Shiga, Wakayama,
Hyogo, Mie (Kansai area), and across Japan.
Purchase：Discount transportation passes, JR
passes, Day-trip tours, Admission tickets, SIM cards
Accommodations：Make reservations
Services：Free Wi-Fi & Internet, ATM, Money
exchange machine (12 types of currency), Japanese
culture experiences, information, events, and prayer
room
Languages：English, Chinese and Korean.
Luggage：Same-day luggage delivery to your hotel
in Kyoto, and other delivery services, Temporary
luggage holding
Address：3F Kyoto Tower, 721-1 Higashi-shiokōji-
chō, Shichijō-saguru, Karasuma-dōri, Shimogyō-ku,
Kyoto City
☎075-341-0280　FAX075-341-0281
Hours：10:00～18:00 < Closed from December 30 to
January 3>
http://www.tic-kansai.jp/kyoto/

【KYOTO CITY TOURISM ASSOCIATION】
KYOTO CITY TOURISM ASSOCIATION manages
tourism projects, promoting the many tourist
attractions of Kyoto. In addition to providing tourist
information, the association also carries out
publicity inside and outside Japan to raise
awareness of Kyoto.
☎075-752-7070　http://www.kyokanko.or.jp/

【Kyoto Official Travel Guide 】
Website for Kyoto Tourism
http://kyoto.travel/en

TOURIST SERVICES

無料公衆LAN「KYOTO Wi-Fi」
京都市と連携した事業者が提供するWi-Fiサービス。無
料で、24時間利用できる（市バス停では深夜1:00～5:
00は除く）。

歩くまち京都アプリ「バス・鉄道の達人」
市内を運行するバス・鉄道による目的地までの経路や所
要時間を調べられる無料アプリ。
http://www.arukumachikyoto.jp/index.
php?lang=ja

Free Wi-Fi Service
KYOTO Wi-Fi is the free Wi-Fi service offered by Kyoto
City and business partners.
http://kanko.city.kyoto.lg.jp/wifi/en/
http://www.kyoto.travel/kyoto_wifi.html

City Buses and Rail Services
The Arukumachi KYOTO App is an easy-to-use free
search application offering information on available
routes, timetables and fares for city buses and rail
services in Kyoto City, simply by entering departures
and destination.

「Kyoto Fan」
Discover Kyoto 編集部

2011年に立ち上げたDiscover Kyoto編集部（株式会社 俄）のFacebookページ「Kyoto Fan」は、外国人ならではの斬新な目線で京都の奥深い魅力を取材し、現在、世界の320万人が読む大人気ファンページとなっている。その成長に伴い編集部も拡大し、現在はイギリス、ニュージーランド、オーストラリア、タイ、アメリカから京都に移り住んだ5人のメンバーで制作。2015年冬には公式サイト「Discover Kyoto」を開設予定。

Conceived in 2011, NIWAKA Corporation's Discover Kyoto team is dedicated to covering the most interesting aspects of Kyoto and sharing them with the world, with current operations run by five members living in Kyoto who hail from England, New Zealand, Australia, Thailand, and America. The next project is the official website Discover Kyoto, projected to open in the winter of 2015.

デザイン／町田　了
文・撮影／Discover Kyoto 編集部（株式会社 俄）
編　　集／五十嵐佳世、中野弘子
　　　　　江崎　泉、荒川陽平
翻　　訳／株式会社トランネット（難波道明）
地図製作／株式会社小学館クリエイティブ
制　　作／望月公栄、太田真由美、星一枝
販　　売／中山智子
宣　　伝／松本浩一

SHOGAKUKAN SELECT MOOK
世界の320万人が“👍いいね!”した
「アメージング京都」
2015年10月6日　初版第1刷発行

著　者　Discover Kyoto編集部（株式会社 俄）
発行者　藤田基予
発行所　株式会社小学館
　　　　〒101-8001　東京都千代田区一ツ橋2-3-1
編　集　03-3230-9773
販　売　03-5281-3555
印　刷　大日本印刷株式会社
製　本　牧製本印刷株式会社

京都マップ　Kyoto Map

京都北部 Northern Kyoto

嵯峨野 Sagano

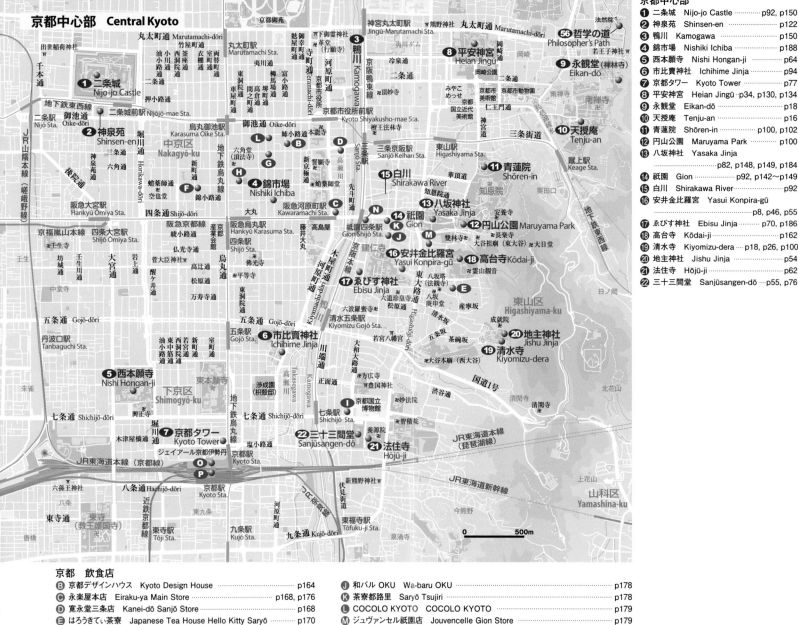

京都中心部　Central Kyoto